CW01659153

# WONDERFUL WORKS OF WOMEN

Joyce Ama Mensah

Paperback ISBN: 978-1-0684708-0-6

For more information about this book see www.jochebedpublishing.com

Email: books@jochebedpublishing.com

# DEDICATION

I dedicate this book primarily to my dear mother, Araba Nkransema Taylor, who raised her children with unconditional love, purposeful guidance and wise counsel. These qualities formed a secure base for my development and inspired me to be the woman that I have become. Many mothers have done exceptionally well, but Araba Taylor surpasses them all.

To my humble-courageous daughter, Joyce Patience Mensah – JOY, for her unwavering support and technological expertise in finding and bringing together all the missing pieces of the jigsaw to complete this project so beautifully – as her 'Wonderful Works' contribution.

# CONTENTS

# FOREWORD

I wish this little book of Joyce's had been available 30 years ago as I entered pastoral ministry – it would have spared me several awkward situations and corrected some wrong preconceptions about the role of women in the Kingdom of God as seen in the life of the church. My first pastorate was at Pollards Hill Baptist Church in Mitcham, Surrey, where Joyce and her husband Isaac were amongst the membership, along with strong contingents from Ghana, Nigeria, West Indies, Sierra Leone and Zimbabwe – from 1997 to 2007 I observed at first hand the strength and the influence of strong women of God as we travelled together on the journey of "Sharing the Love of Jesus" as per our mission statement. More often than not it was these strong women who rolled up their sleeves and got involved in the ministries of the Church, some of which I was delighted to read are still operating today.

Joyce was – and still is – one of those strong women, wearing her faith openly in every area of her life as a specialist nurse in the renal department of one of our local hospitals. Her bright personality underscored a steely resolve to let people know about Jesus whenever she got the opportunity;

and maybe she could add a chapter about her encounters with one George Best when he was one of her patients and she shared her faith with him.

This book is not simply something theoretical to Joyce – it's a labour of love, and a reflection of her own commitment to and love for the Lord Jesus Christ. In its pages you will find easily accessible descriptions of the faithful women of faith found in the Bible and beyond, some of whom deserve a greater recognition than they have been given. And in a challenge to "The Patriarchy" Joyce makes it very clear that God calls women just as He calls men into ministries for His Kingdom, placing them in leadership roles in both society and Church. Sadly, even today there are some churches and organisations that refuse to see this, and I believe they are the poorer for it.

I thank God for Joyce, for her faith, her commitment, her enthusiasm, and her passion – and am honoured to have been able to work alongside her for those ten years, and now to commend this book to all who pick it up. Buy it, read it, give it to your church leader or to any woman who needs encouraging in her calling from God.

***Rev Martin Ceaser***

# INTRODUCTION

In writing this book, I aim to tell about the wonderful works of women through the supremacy, steadfast love, sovereignty, supernatural ability and great faithfulness of God, the creator of the universe and all that dwell in it. I have recounted Bible stories about ordinary women who did extraordinary things through the power of God in obedience, love and unwavering faith. Also mentioned are women outside the Bible, who have served the Lord and humanity with their God-ordained gifts and talents in the most awesome and marvellous ways. I have highlighted the exceptional ministries of these women to inspire everyone who reads their remarkable stories to feel able and willing to seek, discover, develop and walk in their own dreams, for their unique God-assigned purposes and plans in due time. All things are possible to those who believe (Mark 9:23).

Two Bible passages in particular motivated my writing. The first one is Ephesians 2:10: '*For we are God's workmanship (handiwork), created in Christ Jesus to do good works, which God prepared in advance for us to do.*'

Scripture is clear that God the heavenly Father '*chose us in Him before the creation of the world to be holy and blameless in His sight*', meaning that He had intimate knowledge of us – and a plan for us – before our existence in this world (Ephesians 1:4,11).

David, whom God described as *'a man after my own heart'* (1 Samuel 13:14; Acts 13:22), said, *'All the days ordained for me were written in your book before one of them came to be' (Psalm 139:16).*

These scriptures confirm what God told the prophet Jeremiah when He called him: *'Before I formed you in the womb I knew you, before you were born I set you apart; I appointed you as a prophet to the nations'* (Jeremiah 1:5).

God predestined, called, justified and glorified everyone who would believe in Him by faith, adopting them as sons through Jesus Christ, the image of the invisible Father and the firstborn of all creation. This is in accordance with His plan of working out everything in conformity with the purpose of His will.

However, God is able to work through all His creation, animate and inanimate, to declare His glory, supremacy and majesty (Psalm 19:1-4; Numbers 17:8).

He proclaimed:

> *I am God, and there is no other. I am God and there is none like me.*
> *I make known the end from the beginning, from ancient times what is still to come.*
> *I say, my purpose will stand and I will do all that I please.*
> *From the East I summon a bird of prey;*
> *From a far-off land, a man to fulfil my purpose.*
> *What I have said that I will bring about.*
> *What I have planned that I will do.*
> *Isaiah 46:9-11*

So, the wonderful works of the matriarchs mentioned in this book hinged on His perfect plans and purposes. Their great accomplishments were grounded in their believing and trusting the only one true God. They were willing to surrender in humility and reverence, and to seek His Kingdom first, knowing that *'Unless the Lord builds the house, the builders labour in vain. Unless the Lord watches over the city, the guards stand watch in vain'* (Psalm127:1).

This leads to the second key Bible passage: *'It is God who works in you to will and to act in order to fulfil his good purpose'* (Philippians 2:13).

God carefully created every individual intricately for a specific purpose and with a unique assignment to prepare His people for works of ministry *'so that the body of Christ may be built up until we all reach unity in the faith and in the knowledge of the Son of God'* (Ephesians 4:11-13).

Collectively, all Christians have been entrusted with the gospel and commissioned to *'Go therefore and make disciples of all nations'*, for the establishing of His kingdom here on earth (Matthew 28:19). This calls for boldness, sacrifice and denial of self as we embark on sharing the good news of the gospel with the world. By His abundant grace and loving-kindness, God has given specific gifts and talents to each person, so that everyone has something to contribute to the great commission, for the edification of the church (Romans 12:6-8; 1 Peter 4:10).

These two scriptures have inspired me, as a living testimony to God's faithfulness and His perfect work of grace through Christ, to identify and share other people's miraculous life encounters and achievements through my writing to His glory and honour. It is therefore my earnest prayer that the stories and testimonies in this book will stir your heart and encourage you to discover your God-ordained potential, and align your desires with His will for you by faith, which comes from hearing the word of God (Romans 10:17).

I also pray you will trust that the infallible word of God has the power to divinely assist you to do all things through Him who gives you the ability. His gentle promptings within you will illuminate and direct your paths toward His perfect will for your life (Psalm 119:105, 130; Isaiah 30:21).

The Bible says,

> *Everyone who calls on the name of the Lord will be saved. How then, can they call on the one they have not believed in? And how can they believe in the one of whom they have not heard? And how can they hear without someone preaching to them? And how can they preach unless they are sent?*
> *Romans 10:13-15; Mark 16:15*

> *Everything in this world and beyond comes from God;*
> *Everything exists by His will and His mighty power.*
> *Everything is intended by His sovereignty and for His glory.*
> *Without Him nothing was made that has been made.*
> *From Him and through Him and to Him are all things.*
> *For in Him we live and move and have our being.*
> *To Him be the glory forever!*
> *John 1:3; Romans 11:36; Acts 17:28*

# WHAT DOES THE BIBLE SAY ABOUT A WOMAN?

She is a beloved daughter of God, the Heavenly Father.
(John 1:12-13, Acts 17:28, Romans 8:16-17, Galatians 4:6-7, 1 John 3:1-2)

She is the Creator's treasured masterpiece and His unique Friend.
(Psalm 139:13-16; Job 10:10-12, Jeremiah 1:5, John 15:15, Ephesians 2:10)

She is the crown and glory of the Almighty God, from the beginning of creation.
(Genesis 1:26-27, 2:18, Isaiah 43:7 and 49:16)

She is chosen, cherished and the apple of God the Father's eye.
(John 15:16, 1 Peter 2:9, James 1:18, Ephesians 1:4-5, Zechariah 2:8)

She is the redeemed royalty of His Majesty, the King of kings and the LORD of lords.
(Psalm 103:4, 107:2-3, Isaiah 44:22 and 49:24-26, Ephesians 1:7-8)

# A WOMAN'S MINISTRY

History is replete with evidence of numerous God-loving women who dedicated themselves to serving the purposes of the Lord in their generations with their lives, vocations, time, substance, situations, gifts and talents.

The Bible, the Septuagint and other religious writings have recorded the stories of many faith-filled and courageous matriarchs who served God alongside the patriarchs. These women also served humanity and were recognised as: heroines, prayer warriors, deaconesses, prophetesses, judges, queens, mentors, leaders, apostles, benefactors and fellow workers of God's vineyard.

The women within this narrative lived real lives as daughters, wives, mothers, aunts, sisters, cousins, neighbours, servants, slaves, friends and even harlots.

They lived in predominantly male-dominated societies. However, they emerged with robust courage, determination and dedication to the causes they believed in. Most of them trusted in God with unwavering faith to protect them from social injustices and spiritual adversaries as they navigated life's uncertainties. They faithfully observed God's commandments for their lives, adhering to their own unique inclinations and discerning abilities through the power of the Holy Spirit, who effectually worked in them and propelled them to stand out among the crowd. (Ephesians 6:12, Philippians 2:13)

Some of these women faced belligerent challenges and persecution for taking on roles and positions their societies deemed as inconsistent with their ethnic and cultural identities. They were labelled disloyal to their families, communities, nations and ancestral gods because of their beliefs and responsibilities. As a result, some encountered various punishments such as forced imprisonment, enslavement, divorce, disownment by family, stoning and flogging afflicted by human hands. But most of them, with childlike dependence on the one true God, fought the good fight of faith and prevailed with fasting and unceasing prayer, which they offered both corporately and also independently from the obscurity of their private closets (see Acts 2:42; Revelation 12:11).

# THE FEARLESS AND CONFIDENT WOMAN

## SUSANNA (Daniel 13:1-64 – the Septuagint)

Susanna is described in the Septuagint version of Daniel (chapter 13) as noble, with great beauty, and God-fearing. She was the wife of Joakim, a wealthy and *'most honoured man among the Jews'* in Babylon, and a daughter of Hilkiah (v4).

She was raised according to the Law of Moses by her God-fearing parents who lived just lives in the land of captivity (v2-3). She lived with her husband and children in an expansive house also used as the main courthouse for the Jewish community in Babylon. The community elders, judges and litigants gathered there for the hearing and passing of judgements on all manner of cases. The house was therefore busy with people until the court closed after midday and everyone would leave for their homes. Susanna enjoyed the tranquillity of the evenings in the fair garden joining the house, so she would take the opportunity to walk in nature in her backyard. Two of the community elders, judges in the courthouse, noticed Susanna's beauty as she regularly strolled in her garden and began to secretly lust for her.

One afternoon, after work, these two men bid each other farewell and departed to go to their homes, but they independently detoured back to the garden to carry out their premeditated plans. They then bumped into each other unexpectedly and had to confess the purpose of their mission, agreeing to hide in the bushes to wait for Susanna. It was a very hot day, and Susanna decided to take a bath in the privacy of the walled garden. She sent her maids to get some olive oil and lotion and shut the garden gates. They followed her instructions and then went into the house to fetch the things she wanted. The two elders emerged from their hide-outs as soon as the maidservants had left Susanna. Approaching her, they said: *'Behold, the garden doors are shut, that no man can see us, and we are in love with you. Therefore consent to us, and lie with us. If you will not, we will testify against you, that a young man was with you; therefore you sent your maids away from you'* (v20-21).

Susanna, choosing to abide by the Law of Moses and also to remain faithful in her marriage, answered, *'I am trapped; for if I do this thing, it is death to me. If I don't do it, I can't escape your hands. It is better for me to fall into your hands, and not do it, than to sin in the sight of the Lord'* (v22-23). (See also Leviticus 20:10; Deuteronomy 22:22.)

Susanna's fear of the Lord and her faith in His Word motivated her choice to reject what her society would have accepted as compliance with gender norms. She was not deterred by the rank and authority of her accusers, so she vehemently refused to be coerced by them. Her attitude echoes the psalmist's words: *'The LORD is with me; I will not be afraid. What can man do to me?'* (Psalm 118:6).

She screamed so loud for help that her household rushed into the garden to see what had happened to her. One of the elders discreetly ran to open the garden gates with the intent to frame her for not closing them as she bathed (v25). The two men falsely accused Susanna of committing adultery with a young man who had run off on seeing them. They claimed the youngster was too strong for them to contain. The men were believed because of their influence, position and power. In addition, the Torah states that *'A matter must be established by the testimony of two or three witnesses'* (Deuteronomy 19:15). Susanna's fate was therefore sealed, and she had to face trial the next day in the courts.

Her distraught but supportive family, including her parents and children, accompanied her on the day of her trial. As she stood before the whole assembly, the two judges abashedly unveiled her, laid their hands on her head and pronounced the false adultery charges against her. She was consequently sentenced to death, with no legal obligation to speak or defend herself. Susanna demonstrated steadfast faith, honesty and absolute trust in Almighty God to save her. She looked toward the heavens and cried out loud in prayer, saying; '*Eternal God, nothing can be kept secret from you; you know everything before it happens. Here I am about to die, even though I never did such things as these men have maliciously invented against me*' (v42-43).

Like smoke billowing up from burning incense, Susanna's fervent and conscientious prayers and those of her family throughout her ordeal ascended before the omniscient God.

As she was being led away to be killed, God miraculously answered her prayer. At that eleventh hour, the conscience of a young man named Daniel, who was standing in the assembly, was suddenly stirred by the Holy Spirit, and he cried out with a loud voice, *'I am clear from the blood of this woman!'* (v46).

He then challenged the assembly for being 'fools' and quick to condemn *'a daughter of Israel without examination and without learning the truth'.* This divine intervention prompted a fairer delving into the case, where Daniel was allowed by the assembly to cross-examine the two judges separately. By divine wisdom, his interrogation uncovered serious inconsistencies in the men's accounts of where exactly they saw Susanna and the so-called young man. One of the elders claimed to have witnessed the so-called indecent acts of the accused 'under a mastic tree', while the other stated it was 'under an evergreen oak tree'. The two judges were exposed by the false testimony of their evil and atrocious deeds and were brought to justice. They were punished by the same death sentence that they had passed on Susanna, imposed in accordance with Mosaic law, as laid out in Leviticus 24:19-20.

Their intentions were evil, but God turned the situation around for the good of Susanna, her entire family and all the women in her community who would have fallen prey to those corrupt elders and judges and their insidious injustices. Her courage broke the dead silence of the oppressed woman, who would have stayed silent for fear of stigmatisation and harassment, and whose claims of sexual mistreatment would have been ridiculed and disregarded in a male-dominated society.

She exposed a culture where women's lives were ruled by norms, systems and ideologies that only allowed them few choices with no legal rights. She emboldened and motivated the fearful woman with a voice, through her loud screams and her louder, powerful prayer to God, who promises to answer when we call. This exceedingly great promise of God, as declared in Jeremiah 33:3, came to fruition liberally and abundantly through the activation of Susanna's resolute faith and her knowledge of Deuteronomy 22:24.

Her miraculous victory over her strong enemies testified to her world and to all that:

> *The weapons we fight with are not the weapons of the world. On the contrary, they have divine power to demolish strongholds. We demolish arguments and every pretension that sets itself up against the knowledge of God, and we take captive every thought to make it obedient to Christ.*
> *2 Corinthians 10:4-5*

Her absolute trust in the Lord was rewarded with freedom, unspeakable joy, deliverance and dignity – to the glory of God!

*'Hilkiah and his wife praised God for their daughter Susanna, with Joakim her husband, and all her kindred, because there was no dishonesty found in her'* (v63). The name of the Lord is described in Proverbs 18:10 as a 'strong tower'; *'The righteous run to it and are safe.'*

# THE MINISTRY OF THE OLD TESTAMENT WOMEN

The following women, mentioned in the Old Testament, also prevailed remarkably over crises, temptations, and physical and spiritual enemies throughout their lifetimes. Most of them overcame through their intuitive ability to understand the significance of times and seasons and the importance of obedience to God, and they were attuned to their 'set-time' blessings. They had faith in Yahweh, their ancestral God, as their rock and salvation. They followed His commandments and trusted in His prophets for sound living. God's faithfulness and the assurance of His presence and support were with them always (2 Chronicles 20:20; Deuteronomy 31:8).

## SHIPHRAH AND PUAH (Exodus 1:15-21)

Shiphrah and Puah were the fearless Hebrew midwives who defied Pharaoh's orders to kill the Israelite male babies at birth.

They acted in the fear of God to let the baby boys live (Exodus 1:17).

This happened several years after the death of Joseph when a new Pharaoh assumed the reins of the Egyptian dynasty. He had no knowledge of Joseph, who had served first as a government official and then as second-in-command to his predecessor. He did not care about Joseph's life-saving contribution to the nation of Egypt during the devastating seven-year famine that crippled its surrounding regions. Egypt had been preserved from the famine through Joseph's God-ordained wisdom and intervention. However, as the famine became severe in Canaan, Joseph sought Pharaoh's permission to settle his father Jacob, plus all his brothers and their families (about 70 of them), in the region of Goshen, *'the best part of the land'*; a move God had encouraged Jacob to take in a vision at Beersheba, saying, *'I am God, the God of your father; do not be afraid to go down to Egypt, for I will make you into a great nation there. I will go down to Egypt with you, and I will surely bring you back again. And Joseph's own hand will close your eyes'* (Genesis 46:3-4). (See also 47:1-11 and 27.)

After some time, Joseph's family rapidly multiplied in numbers and strength. The reigning Pharaoh became concerned about the security of his country as the people of Israel continued to increase greatly in number, influence and economic prosperity. He then passed a law to make them slaves and subjected them to forced labour. God had foretold this slavery decree upon the Israelites to Abraham when He made a covenant with him concerning his future uncountable offspring (Genesis 15:13).

In addition to their hard labour, Pharaoh commanded the Hebrew midwives Shiphrah and Puah to kill all the male-born babies of the Hebrew women at birth but let the baby girls live. These two midwives chose to let the boys live because they had a reverential fear of the Lord. Their actions displeased Pharaoh, who summoned them and demanded to know why they had not carried out his order. The midwives defended themselves by saying that the Hebrew women were more vigorous than their Egyptian counterparts and gave birth before the midwives arrived. The Lord blessed the wonderful works of Shiphrah and Puah's hands as the population of the Hebrews continued to increase, despite Pharaoh's ruthless and harsh labour conditions and the economic restrictions imposed on them.

The Lord also blessed Shiphrah and Puah with families of their own and rewarded them with wealth for their faithfulness.

## JOCHEBED (Exodus 2:1-10)

Jochebed, whose name means 'Yahweh is glory', was a descendant of Levi. She was the wife, as well as the aunt, of Amram, and the mother of their three children: Aaron, Miriam and Moses (Exodus 6:20, Numbers 26:59).

She was God-fearing, courageous, intelligent, and an unsung heroine of faith. With a spirit of discernment, she devised a plan to save her baby boy from being killed, following Pharaoh's edict that *'Every Hebrew boy that is born...*

*must be thrown into the Nile, but let every girl live'* (Exodus 1:22).

This decree was intended to limit the prolific growth of the Hebrew population in Egypt. But by her unwavering faith and trust in Yahweh for divine protection, Jochebed hid her baby boy for three months after his birth, because they saw he was no ordinary child, and they were not afraid of the king's edict (Hebrews 11:23).

However, as the boy grew, she could no longer hide him. So, this resourceful mother devised a papyrus basket coated with tar and pitch and placed the child in it. She put it among the reeds along the bank of the river Nile, where he would be seen by people coming to draw water. Miriam, her daughter and the boy's older sister, stood at a distance to see what would happen. The basket eventually fell into the hands of Pharaoh's daughter when she came to the river to bathe. She immediately recognised the baby as a Hebrew child and desired to adopt him. Miriam quickly approached her and confidently offered to get one of the Hebrew women to nurse the baby for her.

Pharaoh's daughter agreed, so Miriam brought along the child's mother, Jochebed, who was offered payment to care for him until he was weaned. After the child was weaned, Jochebed took him to Pharaoh's daughter in the palace, to live as her son. She named him Moses, saying, *'I drew him out of the water'* (Exodus 2:7-10).

Jochebed's faith in the Lord was rewarded, and her heart's desire for her son to live was granted despite Pharaoh's cruel edict.

Jochebed models the rewards of courage and steadfastness in putting our trust and belief in God instead of men. She also portrays the importance and power of fervent prayer as a force that can change a family's trajectory and dynamics, and she displays the unity and strength of a family that prays together. And, as rightly said by Patrick Peyton, 'The family that prays together stays together.' (See also Matthew 18:19-20.)

Jochebed's tenacity to stand for the right, and her godly influence on her children, produced three fearless and devoted leaders in Israel. Her daughter, Miriam, was the prophetess who, after the crossing of the Red Sea, confidently led the Hebrew women in a jubilant celebration of their freedom from Egypt. Jochebed and her family risked their lives to faithfully serve Yahweh as they also sought the well-being of their fellow countrymen. Her two courageous and dedicated sons, Aaron and Moses, stood determined to alter Israel's history through the power of God.

By faith, Moses refused to be known as the son of Pharaoh's daughter when he grew up.

> *He chose to be mistreated along with the people of God rather than to enjoy the pleasures of sin for a short time. He regarded disgrace for the sake of Christ as a greater value than the treasures of Egypt, because he was looking ahead to his reward. By faith he left Egypt, not fearing the king's anger; he persevered because he saw him who is invisible.*
> *Hebrews 11:24-27*

Moses, a living testimony and a fruit of the power of a prayerful mother, boldly stepped into his calling and God's purpose, at the set time, to lead Israel out of bondage.

His brother, Aaron, assisted him in accomplishing that mammoth task in his priestly capacity, as ordained by God, who made it clear to Moses, saying, *'See, I have made you like God to Pharaoh, and your brother Aaron will be your prophet. You are to say everything I command you, and your brother Aaron is to tell Pharaoh to let the Israelites go out of his country'* (Exodus 7:1-2).

Moses was 80 years old and his brother Aaron was 83 when they spoke to Pharaoh (Exodus 7:7). Moses wrote the first five books of the Old Testament, the Pentateuch – Genesis, Exodus, Leviticus, Numbers, and Deuteronomy. He also gave God's own finger-inscribed Ten Commandments on tablets to the Israelites (Exodus 20:1-17).

By faith Aaron, the first son of Jochebed, whose name means 'mountain of strength', 'exalted' or 'strong', became Israel's first priest and the traditional founder of the Israelite priesthood. As a mediator between Yahweh and the nation of Israel, he played a key role in the exodus of Israel from Egypt. He fearlessly spoke to Pharaoh on behalf of his younger brother Moses, as per God's instructions for Israel's liberation from Egyptian slavery. He was tremendously used by God to perform great miracles, some with his Levitical rod/staff, which God endowed with power.

At God's command, Aaron threw his staff down in front of Pharaoh, and it became a snake. Pharaoh's professional sorcerers and wise men, the Egyptian magicians, counteracted by throwing down their staffs, which all became snakes too. But Aaron's staff miraculously swallowed up all the staffs of Pharaoh's magicians (Exodus 7:10-12). Aaron and his sons were instructed by God through Moses to bless the Israelites:

'*The LORD bless you and keep you; The LORD make his face shine upon you and be gracious to you; The LORD turn his countenance toward you and give you peace*' (Numbers 6:24-26). This oft-recited benediction in places of worship is referred to as the 'Priestly' or 'Aaronic' Blessing.

In another development concerning God's heart for Aaron, Korah, a Levite with priestly responsibilities, joined forces with some conspirators to grumble about the extra authority that God had allowed Aaron as high priest and Moses as their leader. They accused them as going 'too far' to lord it over them, but Moses, being certain of their God-given calling, confronted the rebels and said, *'You Levites have gone too far!'* (The whole story is found in Numbers 16.) As a result, God intervened with a plan to resolve the problem of constant grumbling. He commanded Moses to ask the leaders of each of the twelve tribes of Israel to bring their ancestral staff to the tent of meeting, including Aaron's rod, which would represent the tribe of Levi. Each staff had the tribe's name written on it. Moses collected them all, including Aaron's, and placed them before the Lord in the tent of meeting. Then God said to Moses, *'The staff belonging to the man I choose will sprout, and I will rid myself of this constant grumbling against you by the Israelites*' (Numbers 17:5).

The next day, Moses entered the tent and saw that Aaron's staff had not only sprouted but also budded, blossomed and produced almonds! Aaron was vindicated from the conspirators, and he and his descendants became God's unmistakable choice for the responsibilities of high priest.

The Lord told Moses to place Aaron's rod permanently in front of the Ark of the Covenant to serve as a deterrent for the rebels and also to prevent further murmurings and deaths (Numbers 17:1-11; 18:1). Aaron's rod eventually remained in the Ark of the Covenant as a testimony of God's choice of Aaron and Moses to lead the Israelites (Hebrews 9:4b).

## MIRIAM (Exodus 2:4-8, Numbers 12:1-16)

Miriam, Jochebed's astute daughter, was the supportive elder sister of Aaron and Moses. By faith, she offered Jochebed to nurture and raise Moses under the care of his biological family, and in the fear of the Lord, for the benefit of the entire nation of Israel and to the glory of God.

She was the first among the seven prophetesses mentioned in the Bible, and a brave and courageous leader of the women in Israel. After the miraculous crossing of the Red Sea on dry land by the Israelites, Miriam led the women in the celebration procession with her tambourine, and all the women followed her with tambourines and dancing. Then Miriam sang to them, *'Sing to the LORD, for he is highly exalted. The horse and its rider he has hurled into the sea'* (Exodus 15:20-21).

Miriam and Aaron once had to confront Moses about his choice of wife, questioning his spiritual standing as a true man of God. The wife was a Cushite, a non-Hebrew woman, which was against their Jewish religion, and therefore Moses was failing to lead by example (Deuteronomy 7:3-4). However, their resentment and jealousy against Moses's wife appeared bare and unpleasant before omniscient Yahweh. Additionally, their challenges – *'Has the LORD spoken only through Moses?...*

*Hasn't He also spoken through us?'* – displeased the Lord, because they equally questioned His authority and wisdom.

The Lord immediately summoned all three siblings to the tent of meeting, appearing before them in a pillar of cloud to address the issue.

As a consequence, Miriam suffered leprosy the instant the cloud lifted from above the tent. Remorseful, Aaron acknowledged their mistake and pleaded to Moses for mercy. So Moses cried out to the Lord on behalf of his sister, saying, *'Please God, heal her!'* (Numbers 12:13).

By God's command, Miriam was confined outside the camp, where all the other unclean people with defiling skin diseases resided, for seven days, in accordance with the Law (Numbers 5:1-4). The people did not move from where they were in Hazeroth until Miriam was restored and brought back. Then they encamped in the Desert of Paran with her in their midst once again.

The moral of this story is that God is no respecter of persons when it comes to sin (Romans 2:11-13). His ways are not our ways, neither are His thoughts our thoughts, as Isaiah 55:8-9 makes clear. Scripture also teaches that we should love our neighbour as ourselves, as commanded by the Lord through Moses and reiterated by Jesus Christ to his followers (Leviticus 19:18; Mark 12:30-31).

Miriam and her two brothers were great leaders of Israel as a liberated nation. These siblings were the products of a praying, God-fearing and faith-filled mother, Jochebed, whose godly influence shaped their lives. Together, they courageously led the Jewish people for forty years in the desert, despite the harsh murmurings, criticism, betrayal and opposition they faced both outside and inside the camp.

Their faith, dedication and sacrificial services echo the first and second stanzas of Rev. Dr Horatius Bonar's song:

*Go Labour on;*
*Spend and be spent.*
*Thy joy to do the Father's will.*
*It is the way the Master went;*
*Should not the servant tread it still?*

*Go, Labour on:*
*'tis not for nought.*
*Thy earthly loss is heavenly gain.*
*Men heed thee, love thee, praise thee not.*
*The Master praises, what are men?*

## RAHAB (Joshua 2:1-24)

Rahab was a Canaanite woman who lived in Jericho with her family. She is described in Joshua 2:1 as the prostitute who housed two Israelite spies, including Caleb. These men were sent by Joshua to scout out the land, especially Jericho, and bring a report on how Israel would take possession of it. This was in step with God's promise to their ancestors, Abraham and Moses, to give them the land across the Jordan, including every place where they set their feet (Joshua 1:3).

The king of Jericho found out about the presence of the two spies in Rahab's house, so he sent her a demand to give them up, but she denied having them. She had hidden them on her roof and then furnished them with information about the land and how they were to avoid being found by the king's forces. She allowed them to escape by a rope let down from a window, saving them from the wrath of the authorities. Before the men left her house, Rahab demanded an assurance – with signs – that she and her household would be spared when the Israelites eventually returned to possess Jericho. Her outstanding knowledge about the supernatural ability and miraculous deeds of the Israelite God, Yahweh, enabled her to make a faith declaration with conviction: *'I know that the LORD has given this land to you and that a great fear of you has fallen on us, so that all who live in this country are melting in fear because of you… Now then, please swear to me by the LORD, that you will show kindness to my family, because I have shown kindness to you; give me a sure sign…'* (Joshua 2:9-12).

Her request was granted, with a directive from the spies to hang a scarlet cord from the window they had used for escape. She was also instructed to bring all her family members into her household for safety. At the appointed time, and in return for her goodwill, Joshua sanctioned her request, saying, *'Go into the prostitute's house and bring her out and all who belong to her, in accordance with your oath to her' (Joshua 6:22).*

So, by her absolute faith, *'the prostitute Rahab, because she welcomed the spies, was not killed with those who were disobedient'* (Hebrews 11:31).

Rahab's trust in the faithfulness of Israel's covenant-keeping God, the Lord, strong and mighty in battle, inspired her timely response and discerning decision to save the two spies.

Her act of kindness saved her life and those of her entire family, and they lived safely amongst the Israelites.

God rewarded her obedience, as she eventually married Salmon, from the tribe of Judah, and became the mother of Boaz, the kinsman-redeemer who married Ruth the Moabite. Ruth gave birth to their son Obed, who became the father of Jesse, the father of King David. Rahab was not only an ancestor of Israel's great King David but also an ancestor of the Lord Jesus Christ, the Saviour of the world, through His earthly father Joseph (Matthew 1:2-16, Luke 3:23-38, 1 Chronicles 2:11-15).

## DEBORAH (Judges 4;1-24)

Deborah, the wife of Lappidoth, was a fearless military leader and the only female among the twelve judges mentioned in the Old Testament. She was a prophetess whom God divinely endowed with outstanding wisdom, understanding and spiritual discernment to comprehend the move of God.

She confidently and competently performed judicial functions through hearing and resolving disputes among the Israelites, under the Palm of Deborah, situated between Ramah and Bethel in the hill country of Ephraim. Her calling was to lead and guide the people of Israel into ways of righteousness.

She described herself as 'a mother in Israel', who arose when the village life in Israel had ceased before she became a judge (Judges 5:7). Israel's army became too weak to defend its national borders, which resulted in constant harassment and cruel oppression from the neighbouring King Jabin of Canaan for years. God heard Israel's cry for deliverance from their strong enemy and spoke about their imminent deliverance through Deborah. She consequently summoned Barak, the Israelite military commander, and told him that Yahweh, the God of Israel, ordered him to go into battle against Sisera, Jabin's commander. God promised Barak a sound victory over Canaan as an answer to Israel's petition to Him concerning their oppressor.

Barak hesitated and would only go to war if Deborah accompanied him. She agreed, but warned Barak that his request meant that the Lord would award the victory to a woman. Deborah not only suggested the military strategy but also accompanied Barak and his 10,000 soldiers to Mount Tabor to fight against the troops of Sisera, who were advancing with 900 iron chariots. God honoured the word He spoke through the prophetess Deborah for Barak and his men to overwhelmingly win the battle against Sisera's troops (Judges 4:16). (See also Isaiah 55:11.)

## JAEL (Judges 4:16-22)

Jael was a Bedouin, the wife of Heber the Kenite, who had moved from his native land and pitched his tent by the great tree in Zaanannim near Kedesh. During the battle of Mount Tabor, Sisera, the Canaanite army commander, noticed that the tide of the war had turned against him and his troops. He quickly abandoned his 900 iron chariots and his army and fled on foot to seek refuge in Jael's tent, since King Jabin was on friendly terms with her husband's clan. Jael duly met Sisera and welcomed him in.

When Sisera asked her for water to quench his thirst, she gave him curdled milk instead and covered him with a warm rug. He asked Jael to guard the entrance, and not let anyone know that he was hiding there, before falling asleep with exhaustion. Jael did not hesitate to act swiftly on the opportunity she discerned. She took a tent peg and a hammer and went quietly to Sisera, still fast asleep. She drove the peg through his temple, into the ground, and killed him, thus fulfilling Deborah's prophecy that '*the LORD will hand Sisera over to a woman*' when Barak refused to go to war without her. Surely, the Sovereign Lord does nothing without revealing His plan to His servants the prophets! He is faithful to all His promises, and He watches over His word to bring it to pass at the appropriate time. (Amos 3:7, Jeremiah 1:12)

Barak's desperate pursuit of Sisera, the runaway army commander, eventually brought him to Jael's tent. Jael took him inside to witness his opponent's death. Right there before his eyes was the evidence of Deborah's prophecy – he would gain neither the honour nor the credit for Israel's victory over King Jabin's strong army, due to his reticence, lack of self-confidence and lack of faith in the Lord. For: '*Without faith, it is impossible to please God, because anyone who comes to him must believe that he exists and that he rewards those who earnestly seek him*' (Hebrews 11:6).

From then on, the Lord subdued King Jabin before Israel until he was utterly destroyed – another fulfilment of prophecy. Then Israel had peace for forty years (Judges 5:31).

Deborah and Barak praised the Lord with a redemption song, in which the pair honoured Jael as the heroine of the Battle of Mount Tabor:

> *In the days of Shamgar son of Anath, in the days of Jael...*
> *The roads were abandoned; travellers took to winding paths.*
> *Most blessed of women be Jael, the wife of Heber the Kenite.*
> *Most blessed of tent-dwelling women.*
> *He asked for water, and she brought him curdled milk in a bowl fit for nobles.*
> *Her hand reached for the tent peg, her right hand for the workman's hammer.*
> *She struck Sisera, she crushed his head, she shattered and pierced his temple.*
> *At her feet he sank, he fell; there he lay.*
> *At her feet he sank, he fell; where he sank, there he fell – dead...*
> *(Judges 5: 6, 24-27)*

Here, two women with different social statuses and personal capabilities made themselves available for God to use what they had to achieve His purpose for a nation in crisis. Deborah, the ruling judge of Israel, with fearless leadership skills, and Jael, the housewife with bold actions, were brought together by God to redeem Israel from her fierce enemy.

All souls belong to God, therefore He chooses to use whatever or whosoever He may; both the brave and the cowardly, the weak and the strong, the rich and the poor, the uneducated and the elite, the likely and the unexpected, to accomplish His will at the appointed time (Ezekiel 18:4a; Psalm 115:3).

No one is disqualified from God engaging with them. For example, the apostle Paul, originally an arch-enemy of the early Christians, became the greatest ambassador for Christ and wrote a third of the New Testament. He once testified from his prison cell that he had learned how to be content '*in any and every situation, whether well fed or hungry, whether living in plenty or in want. I can do everything through him who gives me strength*' (Philippians 4:12-13).

God infuses strength and power into His Word and makes it available for His service, good pleasure and ultimate purpose. Therefore, '*not that we are competent in ourselves to claim anything for ourselves, but our competence comes from God. He has made us competent as ministers of a new covenant, not of the letter but of the Spirit; for the letter kills, but the Spirit gives life*' (2 Corinthians 3:5-6). The soul that is discerning and sensitive to the Holy Spirit always prevails with the miraculous to the glory and honour of God.

## JEHOSHEBA (2 Kings 11:1-21, 2 Chronicles 22:10-12; 23:1-21)

Jehosheba was the daughter of King Jehoram of Judah and the wife of Jehoiada the high priest of the Lord's temple. She was also half-sister to King Ahaziah, the son of Athaliah, the daughter of King Ahab and Queen Jezebel. When King Ahaziah died, his mother Athaliah ruthlessly proceeded to wipe out all the potential heirs of the ancestral-royal line of

King David, including her own grandchildren, in order to take over the reins of the land. But Princess Jehosheba boldly stepped into her calling, at the appointed time, with a remarkable act of courage to prevent the Davidic lineage from being extinguished.

She fearlessly removed her infant nephew, Prince Joash, son of King Ahaziah, from among the royal princes, who were about to be murdered. She hid him and his nurse in a bedroom in the temple of the Lord and secretly raised him with the help of her husband Jehoiada. Joash remained hidden in the temple for the six years that Athaliah ruled.

In the seventh year and on Joash's seventh birthday, Jehoiada consulted with the Levites of Judah and the heads of Israelite families from all the towns. He made a covenant with them and presented them with the king's son. He put the royal crown on the boy's head and presented him with a copy of the covenant. He also ceremoniously proclaimed him king and anointed him. The people celebrated King Joash's coronation with clapping, praising, blowing of trumpets, and shouts of 'Long live the king!'

When Queen Athaliah heard the shouts of acclamation, she ran to the temple to see for herself. Witnessing her grandson Joash being crowned king as he stood by the pillar, according to custom, with the officers and the trumpeters beside him and all the people rejoicing, she became furious. She tore her robes and called it treason! She tried to fight the situation but was chased away from the temple and overpowered by the soldiers in the palace grounds, where she lost her life.

Joash, whose name means 'given by the Lord', ascended to his rightful place on the royal throne, as king of Judah. All the people of the land rejoiced.

The retention of the Davidic lineage was God's redemption plan, promised to King David through the prophet Nathan: *'Your house and your kingdom will endure forever before me; your throne will be established forever'* (2 Samuel 7:16).

In his old age, Jacob had gathered all his twelve sons and pronounced a blessing on them individually. To Judah, he had said:

> *Judah, your brothers will praise you; your hand will be on the neck of your enemies; your father's sons will bow down to you... The sceptre will not depart from Judah, nor the ruler's staff from between his feet, until he comes to whom it belongs and the obedience of the nations is his.*
> *Genesis 49:8,10*

God always watches over His spoken word and that which is declared in faith, to bring it to pass. He promises to build his church, and the gates of Hades will not overcome it (Matthew 16:18). For example, when Elijah repeated to the Lord that all the prophets of God had been killed, and he is 'the only one left', the Lord astonishingly revealed that, in His sovereignty, He had reserved 7000 in Israel whose knees had not bowed and whose mouths had not kissed Baal (1 Kings 18:22; 19:10,14 and 18).

As the Akan language of Ghana puts it, 'Kataman kita adze a obi nngye', meaning no one can loosen God's grip. He has the final word over all things, and He knows His own. He will always protect his children, whom He describes as the 'apple of His eye', from all evil (Zechariah 2:8).

Jehosheba, whose name means 'the fullness of God', made herself available for God to use her to fulfil His redemptive plan, thus preserving a royal lineage from which our Lord Jesus Christ, the Messiah, would later descend. Her knowledge and understanding of the Word of God perfected her faith and encouraged her timely decision to save her nephew Joash from being murdered by his grandmother.

## SHALLUM'S DAUGHTERS (Nehemiah 3:12)

The torn-down walls of Jerusalem rendered the city defenceless against her enemies. Nehemiah organised and passionately led a team of builders for its restoration. Shallum's daughters were the only women mentioned in the extensive list of the rebuilders of the walls. Their father, Shallum, son of Hallohesh, was a ruler of half the district of Jerusalem, and the Bible records that his daughters played a highly significant role in helping their father to repair their section of the ruined Jerusalem wall. Shallum's daughters' fearlessness, bravery and selfless contribution to the repairing of the walls was remarkable. They worked with their bare hands and feminine strength on the manual job of erecting a fortified city wall.

They risked their lives for the security of their city, the safety of their family and peace of mind for the people of the land.

They were not intimidated by the scale of the opposition, nor the deadly threats to their lives that their work posed. They worked in extremely dangerous situations, where half of the workmen did the work while the other half protected them, equipped with spears, shields, bows and armour (see Nehemiah 4).

They demonstrated that they did not have a spirit of fear, but love for their nation, power in standing with the wall rebuilders by faith, and sound minds to complete the task at hand with nobility. They believed in the supernatural ability and faithfulness of the God they served and were convinced He would protect them against their enemies in due course. God rewards such faith with expected outcomes (2 Timothy 1:7; 1:12; Hebrews 11:6).

# THE MINISTRY OF THE HUMBLE AND COURAGEOUS WOMAN

## TAMAR (Genesis 38)

Tamar was a Canaanite, and the wife of Judah's firstborn son Er, whose life was taken by the Lord for his wicked deeds. Tamar was left a widow and childless.

The law of levirate marriages (see Deuteronomy 25:5-6) ensured the continuity of Tamar's family by her taking her brother-in-law Onan, the second son of Judah, as her next husband. Her father-in-law, Judah, approved it, but Onan resented that any children he bore with her would be seen legally as his brother's.

So, whenever he slept with Tamar, he spilled his semen on the floor to prevent her from getting pregnant. This act was displeasing in the sight of the Lord, so He put Onan to death, leaving Tamar a widow and childless for a second time. Seeing Tamar as a burden to his family, Judah asked her to return to her father's house and live as a widow until his younger son, Shelah, was old enough to marry her. Tamar obeyed and went back to live in her father's household, despite the custom that a widow remained with the family of her husband.

As time passed, Judah lost his wife, and after recovering from his grief, went with his friend Hirah to see the men who were shearing his sheep at Timnah. Meanwhile, Tamar remained a childless widow, with no hope of getting married to Shelah, even though he was now eligible for marriage. Taking matters into her own hands, she devised a plan to take away the shame the Judah family had put her through and to secure her future and dignity in society.

Canaanite sheep-shearing festivals involved worship and ritual prostitution to promote fertility. Therefore, when Tamar heard about her father-in-law's trip to Timnah, she took off her widow's clothes and disguised herself as a temple prostitute, heavily covered with a veil, as they usually were, and sat at the entrance of the road.

Thinking she was a shrine prostitute, Judah approached her.

> *'Come now, let me sleep with you.'*
> *'And what will you give me to sleep with you?' she asked.*
> *'I'll send you a young goat from my flock,' he said.*
> *'Will you give me something as a pledge until you send it?' she asked.*
> *He said, 'What pledge should I give you?'*
> *'Your seal and its cord, and the staff in your hand,' she answered.*
> *Genesis 38:16-18*

The three promissory items Tamar took were all symbols representing Judah's tribal leadership. He willingly gave them to her, then slept with her, and she became pregnant. In the meantime, Judah kept his promise by sending the young goat by his friend Hirah, in order to retrieve his belongings from the woman, but found she had already left to go home.

About three months later, Judah was informed that Tamar, his daughter-in-law, had been guilty of prostitution and was pregnant as a result. Judah, who still held the power to her fate, responded furiously and demanded she be burned to death, according to the law of the land. But before anything could happen to her, she sent a message to her father-in-law, along with the three pledged promissory items, stating that the owner of those items was responsible for her pregnancy: '*See if you recognise whose seal and cord and staff these are.*' On recognising the items from Tamar, Judah readily owned up and confessed by saying, '*She is more righteous than I, since I wouldn't give her to my son Shelah*' (Genesis 38:26).

There were twin boys in her womb at the time of delivery. Zerah, whose name means 'dawning' or 'shining', stuck out his hand first, so the midwife tied his wrist with a scarlet thread, saying, '*This one came out first.*' But Perez was actually the first to be fully born, hence his name, meaning 'breach', 'breakthrough', or 'burst forth'.

The moral of Tamar's story is that people should not rush to judge but first fully understand the reasons behind every desperate situation. It also teaches people to see others as God sees them and assign them their due. Tamar's deceitful action was a violation of God's law, yet, in His sovereignty, God chose to bring about His purposes through such a messy situation (see Psalm 135:6). He was portraying that even when we fail, His purpose for us will still prevail, for His gifts and call are irrevocable (Romans 11:29). His mercy triumphs over judgement. Through the work on the cross, He demonstrated His unconditional love to mankind, in that *'While we were still sinners, Christ died for us'* (Romans 5:8). Therefore, *'It is by grace you have been saved, through faith, and this is not from yourselves, it is the gift of God, not by works, so that no one can boast'* (Ephesians 2:8-9).

When Tamar was faithless and took the matter into her own hands, her unchanging God, Yahweh, remained faithful. All three men involved in her dilemma were judged for their disobedience to God and their mistreatment of her, but she was blessed because the motive behind her audacious action was to maintain her dignity and place in society and to continue the lineage of Judah.

She went on to become an ancestor of our Lord Jesus Christ through her son Perez, whose royal lineage engendered King David, from whom Joseph the husband of the virgin Mary descended (Ruth 4:18-22; Matthew 1:1-17).

## THE DAUGHTERS OF ZELOPHEHAD (Numbers 27:1-11)

The five daughters of Zelophehad were from the clan of Manasseh, through Gilead, the great-grandson of Joseph. Their names were Mahlah, Noah, Hoglah, Milkah and Tirzah. These women brought an unusual legacy issue before Moses, Eleazar the priest and the leaders of the whole assembly, at the entrance to the tent of meeting, concerning their late father's family inheritance. They presented their case like this:

> *Our father died in the desert. He was not among Korah's followers, who banded together against the LORD, but he died for his own sin and left no sons. Why should our father's name disappear from his clan because he had no son? Give us property among our father's relatives.*
> *Numbers 27:3-4*

Being the first case of its kind to be contested in the land, with no precedent in the Law to back their demands, Moses took their request before the Lord in prayer. The Lord deemed their humble request appropriate and answered:

> *What Zelophehad's daughters are saying is right. You must certainly give them property as an inheritance among their father's relatives and turn their father's inheritance over to them. Say to the Israelites, if a man dies and leaves no son, turn his inheritance over to his daughter…*
> *Numbers 27:7-8*

God, the faithful Father and the Good Shepherd, is no respecter of persons and provides for all He has made. He rewarded the bravery and positive intentions of the five sisters, who did not only ask for property but wanted to honour their father by keeping his name in his clan. This test case won a huge victory for all the females in the land, especially those who had been deprived of their rightful inheritance for decades, based on the Law.

These courageous women contested and received their territorial inheritance from their father's lot, as their human right. The previous law gave land as an inheritance for sons only. By faith, these five women, Mahlah, Noah, Hoglah, Milkah and Tirzah, took a bold stance in rewriting the existing Hebrew law by correctly going through the prescribed channels with a review of their father's history. A precedent was set as their request was graciously accepted and granted with the blessings of the Lord. They were elevated to equality with their male counterparts in terms of family wealth, and they stood to be counted worthy of inheriting their late father's property and preserving his name.

The book of Numbers concludes by highlighting the obedience of Zelophehad's daughters, who not only fought for their rightful inheritance but also obeyed God's commands through Moses. They married within the clans of the descendants of Manasseh, son of Joseph, so that their inheritance would remain within their father's clan (Numbers 36:10-12).

## RUTH (Ruth 1-4)

In the days when Judges ruled Israel, around 1200 BC, there happened to be a famine in the land of Judah. This caused a native of Bethlehem in Judah, named Elimelech, to leave his hometown for the foreign country of Moab, along with his wife Naomi and two sons, Mahlon and Kilion.

Not long after their arrival, Elimelech died. The two sons grew up and married Moabite women, Ruth and Orpah. Ten years later, both Mahlon and Kilion also died. Naomi, a believer in Yahweh, felt empty, heartbroken and discouraged and thought that God had dealt harshly with her.

After some time had passed, Naomi heard that the famine in Judah had ended, and God had blessed the people with a good harvest, so she decided to return to her homeland. She left Moab with her two daughters-in-law and set off for the land of Judah. As they journeyed on, Naomi, with mixed feelings of bitterness, disappointment and also profound gratitude to the girls, suggested that they go back to their mothers in Moab and settle down. Then she kissed them goodbye. The girls wept aloud and insisted they were not going anywhere without her. With further persuasion from Naomi, Orpah gave in, kissed her mother-in-law goodbye and returned to Moab, but Ruth held on, despite Naomi's strong insistence that she should go too.

Ruth chose to live the rest of her life with her mother-in-law, without any compromise. The magnitude of Naomi's enormous pressure on Ruth to separate herself from her produced, like a refiner's fire, one of the most passionate and powerful statements of true commitment and love:

> *Don't urge me to leave you or to turn back from you. Where you go I will go, and where you stay, I will stay. Your people will be my people and your God my God. Where you die, I will die, and there I will be buried. May the LORD deal with me, be it ever so*

*severely, if anything but death separates you and me.*
*Ruth 1:16-17*

When they both reached Bethlehem, the Bible says that the whole town was stirred because of them. God surely had a hand in their union, for He works in us to will and to act according to the power that is at work in us, and His purposes always prevail over man's plans (Philippians 2:13; Proverbs 16:9).

Ruth's absolute trust and faith in her newfound God, Yahweh, as well as her selfless care and great love for her mother-in-law, caused her to live in a country where she was seen as an outsider and an enemy. She was also aware that she would not have any social or religious standing in her new environment, because the Law of Moses categorically stated that *'No Ammonite or Moabite or any of his descendants may enter the assembly of the LORD, even down to the tenth generation' (Deuteronomy 23:3).* None of that distracted her focus. She took a huge step of faith in proceeding to Bethlehem, knowing that when a man's ways please the Lord, He makes even his enemies live at peace with him (Proverbs:16:7).

It was the beginning of the barley harvest when they arrived in Bethlehem. Ruth seemed to be well-versed in Mosaic law as regards the provision of food stamps for the poor and the foreigner in the land (Leviticus 23:22). She voluntarily offered to go to the fields and glean behind the harvesters to provide food for herself and her mother-in-law. Her determination and dedication paid off as she found herself in the barley fields of a relative of Elimelech named Boaz, whom the Bible describes as *'a man of standing'* (Ruth 2:1).

Not long after Ruth arrived in the field, Boaz spotted her gleaning behind his harvesters. He asked who she was and then permitted her to glean only from his farms, and he also ordered his workmen to look out for her safety and security. Boaz's remarkable kindness, respect and courtesy overwhelmed Ruth. Bowing down with her face to the ground, she asked him, *'Why have I found such favour in your eyes that you notice me – a foreigner?'* (Ruth 2:10). This question echoes David's words: *'What is man that you are mindful of him, the son of man that you care for him?'* (Psalm 8:4).

Boaz's reply was a testament to Ruth's exceptional diligence, loyalty and faith in Yahweh, coupled with his own personal blessings:

> *I've been told all about what you have done for your mother-in-law since the death of your husband – how you left your father and mother and your homeland and came to live with a people you did not know before. May the LORD repay you for what you have done. May you be richly rewarded by the LORD, the God of Israel, under whose wings you have come to take refuge.*
> *Ruth 2:11-12 (see also Proverbs 22:29).*

A 'good name' is said to be more desirable than great riches, and to be esteemed is better than silver or gold (Proverbs 22:1). The illumination of Ruth's noble character and her teachable attitude shone brightly and marvellously before the eyes of her community. She was highly esteemed by the women in the town as they bore witness to God's favour on her life. This favour caused Boaz not only to invite Ruth to share dinner with him but also to instruct his harvesters to let her gather among the sheaves. Not only that; they were to pull out some stalks from the bundles and leave them for her to pick up, without rebuking or embarrassing her.

He also told Ruth to keep gleaning in his fields until the end of the wheat and barley harvests. The exclusive safety and security measures that Boaz, the generous and considerate boss, accorded Ruth, put her mind at ease and motivated her to go into the field daily to fend for herself and her widowed mother-in-law.

Ruth's courageous humility models the apostle Paul's teachings in his letter to the Philippians, which is also an admonition to every believer:

> *Do nothing out of selfish ambition or vain conceit, but in humility consider others better than yourselves. Each of you should look not only to your own interests, but also to the interests of others. Your attitude should be the same as that of Christ Jesus: Who, being in very nature God, did not consider equality with God something to be grasped, but made himself nothing, taking the very nature of a servant, being made in human likeness. And being found in appearance as a man, he humbled himself and became obedient to death – even death on a cross!*
> *Philippians 2:3-8*

Ruth did not look out only for her own interests. In addition to taking home daily food supplies from gleaning in the fields, she also saved for her mother-in-law part of a cooked lunch that Boaz offered her, thus fulfilling the scripture that *'A generous man will prosper; he who refreshes others will himself be refreshed'* (Proverbs 11:25).

Perceiving that Ruth and Boaz were undoubtedly attracted to one another, Naomi came up with a very clever strategy, based on the Jewish tradition of levirate marriage, to try and find a home for Ruth where she would be well provided for. The levirate obligation required a widow to become the wife of her husband's brother or a close relative in order to produce a child to inherit her late husband's estate, and also to preserve his name (Deuteronomy 25:5). Ruth submitted to the wise counsel and godly mentoring of her mother-in-law by affirming, *'I will do whatever you say'* (Ruth 3:5).

Ruth and Boaz's relationship would eventually blossom into intimate union, but there was another kinsman-redeemer who was next in line – closer than Boaz. To resolve Naomi's plight, Boaz took ten town elders with him to meet with the kinsman-redeemer, as required by Jewish tradition. Ten Jewish adult males are referred to as *minyan* in Hebrew; a quorum that constitutes a representative for liturgical purposes or traditional Jewish worship.

At the meeting, the kinsman-redeemer was given his rightful place to buy Naomi's land and acquire Ruth as his wife, in order to maintain the name of the dead with his property. On hearing that the deal included Ruth, he rejected the offer and passed the honorary position to Boaz as the next in line, saying, *'Buy it yourself,'* and he removed his sandal as a sign of relinquishing his right to redeem (Ruth 4:8).

Boaz readily agreed to act as a kinsman-redeemer by buying Naomi's estate and taking Ruth as his wife, with the ten elders and others as witnesses. Ruth eventually experienced the joy of motherhood as God blessed their union with their son, Obed. The women in the town gave thanks to the Lord and rejoiced with Ruth and Naomi. They highly commended Ruth as being better to Naomi than seven sons. Ruth's loyalty, passionate attitude and commitment brought her affluence and honour within her marriage and wider society. She bountifully reaped the benefit of patience and perseverance, as described in Paul's letter to the Galatian church where he emphasised this in 'large letters':

> *Let us not become weary in doing good, for at the proper time we will reap a harvest if we do not give up. Therefore, as we have opportunity, let us do good to all people, especially to those who belong to the family of believers.*
> *Galatians 6:9-10*

Ruth lived up to the meanings of her name, which are 'mercy', 'companion', and 'vision of beauty'. She led her life through the lenses of love, faith, integrity, dedication, compassion, kindness, obedience, gratitude, generosity and the true worship of God, with all her heart, soul, mind and strength.

Her humility and fear of the Lord brought her wealth, honour and abundant life, through her marriage to her devoted and God-fearing husband, Boaz. She also became a Gentile ancestor of the Lord Jesus Christ, through their son Obed, who became the father of Jesse, and Jesse became the father of King David (Ruth 4:18-22; Matthew 1:1-16). (See also Proverbs 22:4.)

## HANNAH (1 Samuel 1, 2 and 3)

Hannah was married to Elkanah of the tribe of Levi. Elkanah's other wife, Peninnah, had children with him, but Hannah was barren. Elkanah took his two wives and children yearly to the tabernacle at Shiloh, the national place of worship, to sacrifice and worship in honour of his vows to God, as was their tradition (Deuteronomy 16:16-17).

Hannah's barrenness attracted repeated provocations from her rival Peninnah, which continued even as they went up to the house of the LORD at Shiloh. Peninnah would goad Hannah until she wept and would not eat. Hannah became deeply troubled and resorted to praying unceasingly and fervently out of her desperation for a child. Her physical anguish was apparent as she prayed in the tabernacle, with her lips moving but making no sound. Eli, the temple priest, accused her of being drunk and asked her to put away her wine. But Hannah replied, '*Not so, my lord... I am a woman who is deeply troubled. I have not been drinking wine or beer; I was pouring out my soul to the LORD. Do not take your servant for a wicked woman; I have been praying here out of my great anguish and grief*' (1 Samuel 1:15-16).

Eli agreed that Hannah's prayer request be granted by God, and he sent her away in peace. Having received Eli's blessing with faith and gladness, Hannah returned to the feast and was able to eat. When they went back to Raman, the Lord remembered Hannah and she became pregnant. In her prayer request, Hannah had specifically asked the Lord for a son and vowed to give him back to God to serve in the temple. Her prayer was granted. She named her son Samuel, *'Because I asked the Lord for him'* (1 Samuel 1:20).

Hannah gave thanks to the Lord in praise:

> *My heart rejoices in the LORD; in the LORD my horn is lifted high. My mouth boasts over my enemies, for I delight in your deliverance. There is no one holy like the LORD; there is no one besides you; there is no Rock like our God. Do not keep talking so proudly or let your mouth speak such arrogance, for the LORD is a God who knows, and by him deeds are weighed. The bows of the warriors are broken, but those who stumbled are armed with strength. Those who were full hire themselves out for food, but those who were hungry hunger no more. She who was barren has borne seven children, but she who has had many sons pines away. The LORD brings death and makes alive; he brings down to the grave and raises up. The LORD sends poverty and wealth; he humbles and he exalts; he raises the poor from the dust and lifts the needy from the ash heap; he seats them with princes and has them inherit a throne of honour. For the foundations of the earth are the LORD's; upon them*

> *he has set the world. He will guard the feet of his saints, but the wicked will be silenced in darkness. It is not by strength that one prevails; those who oppose the LORD will be shattered. He will thunder against them from heaven; the LORD will judge the ends of the earth. He will give strength to his king and exalt the horn of his anointed.*
> *1 Samuel 2:1-10*

After Samuel was weaned, Hannah fulfilled her vow and gave him up to be raised by the priest Eli, in Shiloh. God rewarded Hannah's faith and her selfless acts of obedience by granting her three more sons and two daughters.

Samuel served with Eli and his two sons, Hophni and Phinehas, at the tabernacle in Shiloh, where the Ark of the Covenant was housed. Samuel grew to become a priest, a seer, and a spiritual and military leader, the last judge of Israel and an attested prophet of God. He anointed the first two kings of Israel, King Saul and King David. The Lord was with him all the way, and He did not let any of his words fall to the ground (1 Samuel 3:19-20).

Samuel's leadership turned the nation of Israel towards Yahweh. Hannah laid a solid spiritual foundation for her son, through her faith and devotion in the Lord, Yahweh, by raising him with godly principles, in line with the scripture that instructs parents to *'train a child in the way he should go, and when he is old he will not turn from it'* (Proverbs 22:6). Hannah was considered one of the seven prophetesses of the Old Testament.

## THE SHUNAMMITE WOMAN (2 Kings 4:8-37)

On one of his frequent journeys throughout the countryside, the prophet Elisha went to Shunem, of southern Galilee, and met with a well-to-do woman, who urged him to stay for a meal. This act of kindness and hospitality became a regular treat for the prophet to enjoy anytime he dropped by. Eventually, this woman suggested to her husband that they *'make a small room on the roof and put in it a bed and a table, a chair and a lamp for him. Then he can stay there whenever he comes to us'* (2 Kings 4:10).

The project went ahead, and their home became a safe haven for the prophet whenever he was in Shunem. When Elisha next returned, he found how far the woman and her husband had gone to provide for him and his needs. Grateful for their generosity and the respect they had for him, the man of God wished to do something in return, though the couple had asked for nothing. His servant, Gehazi, pointed out to him that the couple had no children. Elisha called the woman and prophesied to her, saying, *'About this time next year, you will hold a son in your arms.'* She replied, *'No, my Lord; don't mislead your servant, O man of God!'* (2 Kings 4:16).

Despite her objection to the prophecy, because they were an older couple, she became pregnant and had a baby boy the following year, just as the prophet Elisha had told her. What is impossible with man is possible with God! (Luke 18:27)

Years later, the boy was with his father on the fields when he suffered a severe headache. He was taken home to recover but died on his mother's lap. His heartbroken mother laid his lifeless body on the prophet's couch and set out to go and tell him the devastating news. When she found the man of God at Mount Carmel, she took hold of his feet to tell him what she had already refused to tell Gehazi. When the servant had asked why she was there, she had told him that *'everything is all right'* – just as she had told her husband *'it is all right'* before she left to see Elisha (2 Kings 4:23 & 26).

Out of her desperation, she broke protocol to see the prophet when it was neither the New Moon nor the Sabbath. She was walking by faith and was steadfast in her composure. She sounded confident in God with her responses, since she believed and was persuaded that her God was able to guard whatever she had entrusted to him for any eventuality (2 Timothy 1:12).

Gehazi, believing the Shunammite woman when she said everything was all right, attempted to prevent her from holding onto the prophet, but his master rebuked him: *'She is in bitter distress, but the LORD has hidden it from me and has not told me why'* (2 Kings 4:27). As it says in Deuteronomy 29:29, *'The secret things belong to the LORD our God, but the things revealed belong to us and to our children forever, that we may follow all the words of this law.'*

In her anguish, the Shunammite woman related to Elisha the reason for her mission, adding, *'Did I ask you for a son, my lord? Didn't I tell you, 'Don't raise my hopes?"* (2 Kings 4:28).

Elisha realised that the boy was the reason for her distress. He immediately sent Gehazi to go and put his prophet's staff on the child's face. He did so, but the boy remained lifeless. Meanwhile, the boy's mother refused to leave Elisha until he went with her to take care of the situation at hand. Her actions clearly indicated her absolute faith that God can do the miraculous. Elisha then journeyed with her to Shunem.

When they reached the house, Elisha shut the door on himself and the boy and prayed to the Lord. Then he got on the bed and stretched himself out on the boy, *'mouth to mouth, eyes to eyes, hands to hands… the boy's body grew warm'* (2 Kings 4:34). He repeated it a second time, and then the boy sneezed seven times and opened his eyes. After Gehazi called the mother, Elisha said to her, *'Take your son.'* The woman fell at his feet and bowed to the ground, then she left with her son.

Imagine the overwhelming joy of this unnamed Shunammite woman in seeing her one and only precious son restored to life. How can anyone be silent about such a wonderful miracle? Her entire community must have known that she served a living God, *who is able to do immeasurably more than all we ask or imagine, according to His power that is at work within us'* (Ephesians 3:20). Her generosity and kindness attracted the Lord's blessing on her family and caused them to have a child even in their old age (Proverbs 11:25).

## NAAMAN'S MAIDSERVANT (2 Kings 5:1-19)

Naaman was a highly regarded commander of the army of King Ben-Hadad II of Aram. He was a gallant soldier and was regarded as a great man by his master because, through him, *'The Lord had given victory to Aram… but he had leprosy.'* Naaman's maidservant was a Hebrew who was captured and taken to Aram during the reign of King Joram of Israel. Despite residing in a pagan community, the maidservant kept her faith in Yahweh, her ancestral God, and maintained her belief about leprosy as a vile disease. This young maid boldly testified to her mistress about the supremacy and power of Yahweh concerning the healing of her master Naaman's leprosy, adding, *'If only my master would see the prophet who is in Samaria! He would cure him of his leprosy'* (2 Kings 5:3).

Naaman told his master, the king of Aram, what his maidservant had said, and sought his permission to go to Israel for his healing. The permission was granted with all the necessary arrangements, including a letter from his master to the king of Israel saying: *'With this letter I am sending my servant Naaman to you so that you may cure him of his leprosy'* (2 Kings 5:6).

When Naaman arrived at Elisha's house, Elisha sent a messenger to him saying, *'Go, wash yourself seven times in the Jordan, and your flesh will be restored and you will be cleansed'* (2 Kings 5:10). This infuriated Naaman, and he went away in rage, because he had expected Elisha himself to meet him in person, and *'call on the name of the LORD his God, wave his hand over the spot and cure me of my leprosy.'* He considered too that there were better rivers for washing in than the Jordan, like the Abana and Pharpar in Damascus. He was walking by sight and not by faith, which not only displeased God but also his maidservant.

His despondent servant went to him and said, *'My father, if the prophet had told you to do some great thing, would you not have done it? How much more, then, when he tells you, 'Wash and be cleansed!'* (2 Kings 5:13).

Naaman swallowed his pride and dipped himself in the river Jordan seven times, as the prophet Elisha had instructed, and *'His flesh was restored and became clean like that of a young boy.'* The cleansed and grateful army commander testified to Elisha of the supernatural ability of his God (Jehovah Rophe – the God who heals), saying, *'Now I know that there is no God in all the world except in Israel'* (2 Kings 5:15).

Then he offered Elisha a gift, since prophets are traditionally paid for their services (1Timothy 5:18). But the prophet refused to accept the offer, saying, *'As surely as the LORD lives, whom I serve, I will not accept a thing'* (2 Kings 5:16). Even though Naaman urged him, he still refused. Naaman then demonstrated his sincere desire to worship the only true God, Yahweh, by requesting soil from Israel to take with him to Aram (2 Kings 5:17). Elisha blessed him to go in peace.

The courageous and confident young captive maid was persistent in her belief and obedient to the precepts of God; she did not compromise her faith. With a clear and focused conscience, she overcame the fear of testifying to the supremacy of Yahweh, her ancestral God, in enemy territory. *'For God did not give us a spirit of timidity, but a spirit of power, of love and of self-discipline'* (2 Timothy 1:7).

She revered Yahweh in her heart and was prepared to confess His healing power to her bosses with gentleness, humility and hope that did not disappoint. Her loyalty and submission to her earthly mistress and master accorded her the respect of Naaman, who readily accepted her challenging proposal to seek healing from the one true God, far superior to the pagan gods of Aram.

She deserved a 'Well done, good and faithful servant' from both her heavenly and earthly masters. She is a good role model for her perseverance in faith, her absolute trust in the Lord, and her unashamed testimony about His mighty power, reflecting Paul's declaration that *'I am not ashamed of the gospel, because it is the power of God for the salvation of everyone who believes: first to the Jew, then to the Gentile'* (Romans 1:16).

## ESTHER (Esther 1-10)

Esther, whose Hebrew name was Hadassah, was the orphaned daughter of Abihail of the tribe of Benjamin. Her family was taken captive into exile from Jerusalem by King Nebuchadnezzar of Babylon. She was raised by her older cousin, Mordecai, when she lost her parents in exile (Esther 2:15).

Esther courageously risked her life by breaking a long-standing tradition by going into King Xerxes's presence without requesting an audience. She did so after Mordecai informed her that Haman, the king's court official, had convinced the king to order the annihilation of all the Jews living within the kingdom. Haman promised to put 10,000 talents of silver into the royal treasury for the king's administrators. The king made Haman's proclamation authentic by giving him his ring but urged him to *'Keep the money, and do with the people as you please'* (Esther 3:11).

This atrocious plot to kill the Jews was an act of revenge on Mordecai for refusing to bow to Haman or pay him honour. As a devout Jewish believer, Mordecai's refusal to bow to Haman might have sprung from his obedience to God's commandment that *'You shall not bow down to them or worship them; for I, the LORD your God, am a jealous God'* (Exodus 20:5). However, he reminded Esther of her Jewish heritage and her position as queen:

> *Do not think that because you are in the king's house you alone of all the Jews will escape. For if you remain silent at this time, relief and deliverance for the Jews will arise from another place... who knows but that you have come to royal position for such a time as this?*
> *Esther 4:13-14*

Having pondered Mordecai's statement, Esther decided to take action. She was determined, with a defiant mindset of 'come-what-may', as she made her intentions known to Mordecai: *'I will go to the king, even though it is against the law. And if I perish, I perish'* (Esther 4:16).

In the meantime, Esther directed Mordecai to engage all the Jews in Susa in fasting for three days, along with her and her royal attendants, prior to her approaching the king with her plea for mercy. On the third day of their fast, Esther wore her royal robe and stood in full view of the king on his throne. Pleased to see her, the king held out the gold sceptre for her to draw near, promising to grant her whatever she wanted, even if it were half of his kingdom. God's favour on Queen Esther broke the royal court protocol and ushered her into the realm of possibility.

Nothing is impossible for God to do. He is the one who declared, *'I AM the Lord, the God of all flesh. Is anything too hard for me?'* (Jeremiah 32:27).

Queen Esther responded by extending a special invitation for the king and Haman to attend a banquet the next day. On the second day of the banquet, as they were drinking, the king enquired once more about Esther's petition. She answered:

> *If I have found favour with you, O king, and if it pleases your majesty, grant me my life – this is my petition. And spare my people – this is my request. For I and my people have been sold to be destroyed, killed and annihilated. If we had merely been sold as male and female slaves, I would have kept quiet, because no such distress would justify disturbing the king.*
> *Esther 7:3-4*

When he asked who the perpetrator was, Esther pointed to vile Haman as *'the adversary and the enemy'* (Esther 7:6). That shocking revelation enraged the king and sealed the fate of Haman, who then begged Queen Esther for his life. But it was too late for him, and as Jesus would later admonish Peter in the Garden of Gethsemane, *'the one who lives by the sword dies by the sword'* (Matthew 26:52; see also Leviticus 24:19-20).

By King Xerxes's command, Haman was impaled on the same gallows he had intended for Mordecai. That same day, the king gave Queen Esther Haman's estate as restitution for the offence against her, and she appointed Mordecai over it. The king also instructed Mordecai to write another decree in his name, overruling Haman's death threats against the Jews. This latest edict changed the course of history, and the Jews were miraculously exonerated. Queen Esther became the channel of God's favour over a situation that God Himself had already planned to bring to pass. He communicated His deliverance plan for the Jewish exiles – to bring them back to Jerusalem after 70 years in captivity – through the prophet Jeremiah, who also informed the surviving elders, priests, prophets and all God's people carried into Babylon in a letter (see Jeremiah 29).

God worked His divine plan through Mordecai's position as the palace gatekeeper and also as a man with fatherly influence on Esther. He divinely raised Esther as the queen to King Xerxes in order to fulfil His *good promise* of keeping the exiles alive and bringing them back to Jerusalem at the appointed time, with plans to prosper and not to harm them, plans to give them hope and a future (Jeremiah 29:11).

God's supremacy and Esther's courage, humility and submission were the highlights of this queen's life, even though this book of the Bible, Esther, falls short of mentioning God's name in its entire contents.

What the Lord said about Jeremiah, *'Before I formed you in the womb I knew you, before you were born I set you apart; I appointed you as a prophet to the nations'* (Jeremiah 1:5), also reflected Esther's life. It was *'not by might nor by power'*, but by the ultimate purpose of the Lord, that Esther, the orphaned foreigner and ordinary young woman, was set apart, appointed, called and equipped with heavenly wisdom and a blessing that made her win *'the favour of everyone who saw her'*, including the king who was attracted to her *'more than to any of the other women'* (Esther 2:15 and 17), to save the lives of the exiled Jews in Babylon.

# THE MINISTRY OF THE VIRTUOUS WOMAN (Proverbs 31:1-31)

The wisdom of the virtuous woman in Proverbs chapter 31 is captured in the earnest words King Lemuel's wise mother taught him. She addressed him as *'son of my womb!'* and *'the answer to my prayers!'* This keen mother sought the Lord for her son Lemuel, whose name means *'belonging to God'*, and He answered her. She raised her son by instilling in him godly values of respectful conduct, a heart for the destitute, and how to find and value a noble wife (Proverbs 31:1-9).

The virtuous woman, also referred to as the 'Proverbs 31' woman, is one who demonstrates wisdom in her undertakings. The Bible describes her as *'a wife of noble character, who is worth far more than rubies'* (Proverbs 31:10).

Her husband has full confidence in her because she is trustworthy and God-fearing. She consistently earns him respect in the community where he sits among the elders of the land, echoing the saying, 'Behind every successful man is a woman.' He appreciates and praises her, and so do her children, who also call her blessed. She is a devoted homemaker who nurtures her children with wise counsel and trains them in the way they should go. She adequately feeds her household and cares for their well-being, especially in bad weather conditions, where she provides them with appropriate clothing. She intentionally watches over the affairs of her household with faithful instructions and leaves no room for idle talk or godless chatter (see 2 Timothy 2:16).

She is an excellent housekeeper, who establishes her home with rare and treasured tapestries and godly virtues of unconditional love, joy, peace, patience, kindness, goodness, faithfulness, gentleness and self-control (Galatians 5:22). She is a tree of life and a great source of comfort for those around her.

The virtuous woman is a resourceful and prudent investor, who possesses a fair sense of discernment about her business. She diligently makes linen garments with her own hands and pays attention to detail for quality and profitable products. She sells them and supplies the merchants with sashes. She subsequently re-invests her profits in planting vineyards on fields she carefully considers and buys. She acknowledges her blessings of physical well-being and maintains her energy and strength for her work. She is likened to a merchant ship that brings her food from afar.

She humbly presents herself elegantly in fine linen garments and purple, signifying royalty, wealth and being the 'chosen' of God (1 Peter 2:9). Her inner beauty of integrity, diligence, compassion, dignity and generosity models a life that the Spirit of the Lord rests on; including the Spirit of wisdom, understanding, counsel, might, knowledge and the fear of God (Isaiah 11:2). These qualities define her exquisite beauty, which is of great worth in the sight of the Lord, who looks at the heart of man and gives knowledge to the discerning. The virtuous woman is a role model to emulate for godly and fulfilling living in all relationships (John 10:10).

*'Many women do noble things, but a virtuous woman surpasses them all… Her wonderful works will bring her praise at the city gate'* (Proverbs 31:29,31).

# THE MINISTRY OF THE GOSPEL-CENTRED WOMAN

The New Testament records some wonderful works of enthusiastic and devoted gospel-centred women. They willingly embraced and fearlessly proclaimed the gospel message of grace, mercy and love to their generations. They also rose above their society's disparaging attitudes towards women, as well as the stereotypical traditions of female subordination, to carry out their God-ordained callings. They publicly demonstrated their commitment and were devoted to specific ministries as co-workers for the gospel according to their spiritual gifts.

They followed on through Jesus's crucifixion, celebrated His victorious resurrection, witnessed His ascension and received the baptism of the Holy Spirit on the day of Pentecost, which marked the beginning of the Christian church's mission to the world (Matthew 27:55-56; Acts 1:14; 2:1-21).

Before His ascension to heaven, Jesus met with His followers, including His 11 disciples, on the Arbel mountain.

By the divine authority over heaven and earth given to Him by God the Father, He commissioned all his followers to *'go and make disciples of all nations, baptising them in the name of the Father and of the Son and of the Holy Spirit'* (Matthew 28:19-20). The women believers got involved with this mandate willingly and with obedient hearts. They took the gospel message and unashamedly proclaimed it in the power of the Holy Spirit, who gave them the strength, courage, knowledge, wisdom and love to win souls for God's kingdom (Acts 1:8).

The innate nature of women as nurturers strategically positioned and enabled them to influence their relations, communities, nations and families with God's message of redemption and reconciliation. They resolutely devoted their time and resources to work in unity with the disciples in promoting the good news.

With great endurance and faith, some of these women sacrificially offered their homes for hospitality, worship and instruction for godly lives. They wholeheartedly served the Lord and humanity with their respective wealth, influence, spiritual gifts and talents (Romans 16:1-16; Acts 12:12; Colossians 4:15; Philemon 1:2).

## MARY, MOTHER OF JESUS (Luke 1:26-38)

Mary, from Nazareth, was a virgin chosen by God to become the mother of Jesus Christ, His son, by divine assignation. She was a teenager who had been betrothed to Joseph, a descendant of King David. In the sixth month of her cousin Elizabeth's pregnancy with John the Baptist, Mary had a visitation from the angel Gabriel. His greeting told her she was *'highly favoured'* and the Lord was with her. Mary was troubled, but the angel allayed her anxiety by reassuring her that she had 'found favour with God' and was going to be pregnant with a son whom she should name Jesus. The angel added that the child would be great and be called *'the son of the Most High'*, and that God would give him the throne of his father David and His kingdom would never end. Mary wondered how this would happen since she was a virgin. But the angel continued to explain to her that she would conceive when the Holy Spirit came upon her and the power of the Most High overshadowed her. Mary's humble response to the message was, *'I am the Lord's servant; may it be to me as you have said'* (Luke 1:38).

When the angel left, Mary set off to visit Elizabeth in Judea, instinctively sensing she needed to share her distinctive and life-changing story with another 'miracle mother'. She needed the right environment to nurture her noble calling, and Elizabeth provided that spiritual guidance and encouragement. Deep called to deep as the two faith-filled believers met. On Mary's arrival, Elizabeth's soul was stirred to recognise her as the 'mother of God'. Filled with the Holy Spirit, she made a loud proclamation, in confirmation of the angel's annunciation, saying, *'Blessed are you among women, and blessed is the child you will bear! But why am I so favoured that the mother of my Lord should come to me?'* (Luke 1:42-43).

Subsequently, Mary herself burst into thanksgiving and praised God for His faithfulness and His blessings upon her with the words of the Magnificat:

*My soul glorifies the Lord; my spirit rejoices in God my Saviour.*
*For he has looked with favour on his lowly servant.*
*From this day all generations will call me blessed:*
*For the Almighty has done great things for me; Holy is his Name.*
*He has mercy on those who fear him from generation to generation.*
*He has performed mighty deeds with his arm,*
*He has scattered those who are proud in their inmost thoughts.*
*He has brought down rulers from their thrones but has lifted up the humble.*
*He has filled the hungry with good things but has sent the rich away empty.*
*He has helped his servant Israel, remembering to be merciful to Abraham and his descendants forever, even as he said to our fathers.*
*Luke 1:46-55*

Mary demonstrated here her knowledge of God's promise to be merciful to His chosen people Israel, through Abraham, and of Him keeping His covenant of love to a thousand generations (Deuteronomy 7:9). This concept must have unveiled Mary's discernment of God's unmerited favour upon her life. She therefore embraced the divine assignation with faith and humility. Her willingness to answer God's call birthed her own resounding 'Yes-Ministry' through which God set in motion His eternal plan to come down to earth and reconcile mankind to Himself (Colossians 1:19-20).

When Mary became pregnant with Jesus, Joseph decided to break off the engagement quietly, but the Lord told him in a dream that Mary's conception was a miracle of the Holy Spirit. Mary was steadfast in her calling as a mother to Jesus from the moment of His conception and His birth in the stable at Bethlehem. She wrapped her baby in a swaddling blanket and laid him in a manger because there was no place for them in the inn when they arrived, at Caesar Augustus's decree, from Nazareth of Galilee (Luke 2:1,7).

An angel of the Lord first announced Jesus's birth to nearby shepherds taking care of their flock. They left their sheep and went to see Him lying in a manger, affirming the sign given to them by the angel. They spread the message about the arrival of the Messiah, Christ the Lord. All who heard the news were amazed, but Mary treasured all these things and pondered them in her heart.

On the eighth day, when it was time to circumcise Him, He was named Jesus, just as the angel had said before His conception. When their purification had been completed, according to the Law of Moses concerning every firstborn male, Joseph and Mary took Jesus to the temple in Jerusalem to present Him to the Lord.

When Jesus turned twelve years of age, Mary and Joseph took him to Jerusalem for the Festival of the Passover, as was their custom. After the festival was over, Jesus stayed behind in Jerusalem, but His parents were not aware until they had been travelling homeward for a whole day. They hurriedly returned to Jerusalem and after three days found Him in the temple courts. He was sitting among rabbis and teachers of the Law, listening and asking questions with profound knowledge, wisdom and understanding. His awestruck mother asked, *'Son, why have you treated us like this? Your father and I have been anxiously searching for you'* (Luke 2:48). Jesus's response, that He was about His 'Father's business', proved He was aware of who He was – the promised Messiah – and that He was anxious to take on the divine commission. However, with obedience, Jesus went back to Nazareth with His parents, submitting to their authority.

He worked alongside His earthly father Joseph, a carpenter, for 18 years, as He waited patiently for the appointed time to begin His God-ordained ministry. *'And He grew in wisdom and stature and in favour with God and man.'* Once again, His mother Mary *'treasured all these things in her heart'* (Luke 2:51-52).

As the mother of God, Mary universally loved and cared for the well-being of people around her. She was at a wedding in Cana of Galilee with Jesus and His disciples when the party ran out of wine. When Mary informed Jesus, *'They have no more wine,'* Jesus replied, *'Dear woman, why do you involve me? … My time has not yet come'* (John 2:4). Nevertheless, Mary told the servants at the ceremony to do whatever He told them to do. She mindfully encouraged the servants to listen, trust and obey Jesus's trustworthy commands. Eventually, Jesus asked the servants to fill six stone water jars to the brim with water. (According to the Bible, each stone jar could hold 20 to 30 gallons.) Jesus then asked the servants to draw some out and take it to the master of the banquet.

When the master tasted the water that had been turned into wine, he said, *'Everyone brings out the choice wine first and then the cheaper wine after the guests have had too much to drink;*

*but you have saved the best till now'* (John 2:10). This was Jesus's first miracle that revealed his power, authority and glory.

Mary was a faithful wife to Joseph and a caring mother to Jesus and his brothers, James, Joseph, Judas, Simon and Jude, and also his unnamed sisters (Mark 6:3; Jude 1). She was also a very committed, supportive and devoted follower of Jesus during His earthly ministry. At His crucifixion, when Jesus saw His mother and the disciple whom He loved, John, standing nearby, He honoured Mary by placing her in John's care, saying, *'Woman, here is your son,'* and to John, *'Here is your mother.'* From that day on, the disciple took Mary into his home (John 19:26-27).

After Jesus's ascendance to heaven, Mary continued to join in prayer with the disciples, the women believers and Jesus's brothers in Jerusalem, where they stayed and waited for the outpouring of the Holy Spirit (Acts 1:14).

## ELIZABETH (Luke 1:5-25)

Elizabeth, Mary's relative, was the wife of the priest Zechariah and a descendant of Aaron. The Bible describes both Elizabeth and her husband as being *'upright in the sight of God, observing all the Lord's commands and regulations blamelessly'* (Luke 1:6). Elizabeth and Zechariah were childless until they were advanced in age. One day, as Zechariah was performing his priestly service of burning incense in the temple, the angel of the Lord appeared to him and said, *'Do not be afraid, Zechariah; your prayer has been heard. Your wife Elizabeth will bear you a son, and you are to give him the name John'* (Luke 1:13).

Zechariah doubted Gabriel's miraculous message and, as a result, remained unable to speak until the time appointed for Elizabeth to give birth. Meanwhile, Elizabeth praised the Lord, saying, *'In these days he has shown his favour and taken away my disgrace among the people'* (Luke 1:25).

When her son was delivered, her neighbours and relatives heard that the Lord had shown her great mercy, and they rejoiced with her. Like her cousin Mary, Elizabeth's son, who would grow to become John the Baptist, was a fulfilment of God's divine plan of redemption for His children, as prophesied by Isaiah and Malachi long before John was born. He was sent by God to announce the coming of the Messiah, and to preach the message of repentance (Isaiah 40:3, Malachi 3:1).

Elizabeth was the first to recognise Mary as the mother of the Messiah, when her baby, John, leapt inside her womb as Mary greeted her on arriving for a visit. Elizabeth was consequently filled with the Holy Spirit, and she prophetically exclaimed with a loud voice:

> *Blessed are you among women, and blessed is the child you will bear! But why am I so favoured, that the mother of my Lord should come to me? As soon as the sound of your greeting reached my ears, the baby in my womb leaped for joy. Blessed is she who has believed that what the Lord has said to her will be accomplished!*
> *Luke 1:42-45*

Elizabeth's pronouncements of blessedness over Mary, as the chosen vessel to bear the Lord, and her own humble gratitude to God for being a witness to such a miracle, inspired and encouraged Mary to profusely praise and worship the Lord with the words of the Magnificat, which echoes Hannah's prayer in 1 Samuel 2:1-10. This revelation about Jesus as the Lord was later confirmed by His disciple Peter, having been asked who people, including themselves, were saying He was. Peter answered, '*You are the Christ, the Son of the living God*' (Matthew 16:16).

Elizabeth was an encourager and a spiritual mentor to her younger relative. She welcomed Mary into her home and shared hospitality and wise counsel with her for three months. '*As iron sharpens iron, so one man sharpens another*' (Proverbs 27:17).

## ANNA (Luke 2:36-40)

Anna, described in the Bible as a prophetess, was the daughter of Phanuel, of the tribe of Asher. She devoted herself to living and serving continually in the temple after losing her husband of seven years. She was now 84 years old and worshipped night and day, with fasting and prayer, in great anticipation of the Messiah, as foretold by the prophets Isaiah and Micah (Isaiah 9:6; Micah 5:2).

During Jesus's consecration ceremony at the temple, Anna watched as Simeon, the '*righteous and devout*', was moved by the Holy Spirit to take the child Jesus in his arms and then to praise God: '*Sovereign Lord, as you have promised, you may now dismiss your servant in peace. For my eyes have seen your salvation, which you have prepared in the sight of all nations, a light for revelation to the Gentiles and for glory to your people Israel'* (Luke 2:29-32).

Knowing in her heart that the Messiah had come, Anna came up to them, gave thanks to God and spoke about the child Jesus to all who were looking forward to the redemption of Jerusalem. Anna represents patience in waiting. She allowed patience to finish its work in her anticipation for the Saviour of the world (James 1:4).

## SALOME (Matthew 20:20-28)

Salome was the wife of Zebedee and the mother of James and John, whom Jesus nicknamed the 'sons of thunder' for being bold, fierce and loyal disciples (Luke 9:51-56). James and John were not only among Jesus's twelve apostles, but they, with Peter, were the closest to Jesus – His inner circle. They therefore had the exclusive privilege of experiencing some of the most significant moments of Jesus's earthly ministry, like the raising of Jairus's daughter, thus witnessing firsthand the Lord's power over death. They also saw Jesus's transfiguration, where they caught a glimpse of the glory of God's kingdom shining through Him, with the appearance of Moses representing the Law, Elijah representing the prophets and Jesus Himself as the hope of glory and the living Word. This was in fulfilment of the prophets and the Law (Matthew 5:17; 17:1-9; Mark 9:2-9; Luke 9:28-36).

Salome was the ambitious mother who knelt down before Jesus and requested that her sons James and John be given places of honour, with one sitting at His right hand and the other at His left in paradise. Even though Jesus acknowledged that her sons would indeed drink from His 'cup' (representing His great suffering and death), their positions and ranks in the kingdom were up to His Heavenly Father's sovereign choice (Matthew 20:20-23; Acts 12:2).

Salome's remarkable request unveiled a fundamental lesson that Christians must emulate Christ, the Saviour, *'who did not come to be served, but to serve'* (Matthew 20:28). Her son John was the 'beloved disciple' of the Lord Jesus Christ, to whom He entrusted His mother Mary at His crucifixion, so John took Mary into his home to care for her. John also earned the nickname 'the Revelator' for writing the book of Revelation on the island of Patmos, where he was exiled (John 13:23; 19:26-27; Revelation 1:1,4,9).

Salome's passion for the gospel and influence as a godly mother was evident in the lives of her two sons, who dedicated themselves to Jesus and his earthly ministry. She faithfully supported Jesus financially and cared for His needs along with the other female disciples. She also witnessed Jesus's crucifixion and subsequently went to his tomb with Mary Magdalene and Mary, the mother of James and Joseph, when they took sweet spices to anoint Jesus's dead body.

They encountered an angel who asked them why they were seeking the living among the dead and told them that Jesus Christ had risen (Matthew 27:56; Mark 15:40; 16:1).

## MARY, MOTHER OF JOHN MARK (Acts 12:12)

Mary the mother of John Mark is only mentioned once in the Bible, in Acts 12:12. She was a woman of means who lived in Jerusalem. As a generous and faithful believer in Christ, she offered her support in spreading the gospel. She selflessly opened her house as a safe haven for the early Christians to pray, worship and encourage one another in the Lord, without fearing Herod Agrippa, who zealously persecuted the early Christians. He had James the brother of John executed by the sword (beheaded) and imprisoned Peter. After Peter was miraculously broken out of prison by an angel, he walked straight to Mary's house, where the believers had been praying for his release. Mary's devotion and dedication in serving the Lord and the brethren impacted her son John Mark, who served as an assistant, accompanying Paul and Barnabas on their missionary journeys. However, John Mark abandoned them along the way in Pamphylia (Acts 13:13), a behaviour Paul deemed as a mission failure and so refused to allow him back to work on their second mission.

John Mark's action divided Paul and Barnabas, who went their separate ways, but Barnabas, *'son of encouragement',* took John to Cyprus to continue his mission (Acts 15:36-40). Giving John a second chance in missionary services was justified by him becoming a valuable Christian worker by Paul's standards, when he later asked Timothy to *'get Mark and bring him with you, because he is helpful to me in my ministry'* (2 Timothy 4:11).

Furthermore, in Colossians 4:10 and Philemon 1:23-24, Paul endorsed John Mark *'the cousin of Barnabas'* by calling him his 'fellow-labourer'. John Mark's initial in-and-out missionary journeys gave credit to his devoted and faith-filled mother Mary, who raised and trained him in the way he should go, and he did not deviate from it. He became Mark the evangelist, who assisted the apostle Peter with missionary services in Rome and wrote down his sermons. He is the author of the book of Mark, the second gospel, to the glory of God. He produced the harvest of the seed Mark's mother Mary planted in him through her faithful prayers.

## MARY MAGDALENE (Luke 8:1-2; John 20:11-18)

Mary Magdalene was named after the town she lived in, Magdala, on the shores of the Sea of Galilee. She met Jesus in a disturbed state as a demon-possessed individual. Jesus cast from her seven demonic spirits (Mark 16:9). Afterwards, she became a devoted disciple of Jesus, travelling through villages and towns with Him and the other disciples to spread the good news about the kingdom of God.

She also gave financially to support Jesus's ministry. She became a leader among the ministering women and remained faithful and loyal to Jesus when others fled with fear at His crucifixion. She and Mary the mother of James sat together opposite Jesus's tomb (Matthew 27:61, Mark 15:47).

Early the next morning, after the sabbath, she went to the tomb with spices, according to custom, to prepare the Lord's body for burial. She was dismayed to find the tomb empty and wondered where they had taken Him. Her intense sadness and weeping were short-lived, as the two angels at Jesus's tomb asked her, *'Woman, why are you crying?'*

She replied, *'They have taken my Lord away, and I don't know where they have put him'* (John 20:13). Turning around, she came face to face with the risen Christ but took Him to be the gardener. *'Sir, if you have carried him away, tell me where you have put him, and I will get him'* (John 20:15).

Jesus called her name, 'Mary,' then she recognised Him and cried out, *'Rabboni!'* meaning 'teacher'. She drew closer, but Jesus forbade her to touch Him until He had returned to His Father and her Father (John 20:17).

Her faithfulness was immensely rewarded. She was the first to witness Jesus's resurrection and was commissioned by the risen Lord to go and announce His resurrection to the other disciples. So, she went to the disciples and said, *'I have seen the Lord!'* Conveying such a profound message of the risen Lord Jesus Christ earned her the nickname 'the apostle to the apostles'.

Entrusting the resurrection message to Mary Magdalene, as a woman, reassures us that God is the Lord and Father of all. The Master Himself confirmed this in His statement to Mary Magdalene: *'Do not hold on to me, for I have not yet returned to the Father. Go instead to my brothers and tell them, 'I am returning to my Father and your Father, to my God and your God'* (John 20:17-18).

## JOANNA (Luke 8:2-3)

Joanna, whose name means 'Yahweh's gift', was the wife of Chuza, the manager of Herod's household. She was one of the women whom Jesus healed of a disease that controlled her. She had a luxurious lifestyle because of her husband's employment status and wealth, but she risked her comfortable living and openly followed Jesus. In particular, she did not let her association with Herod's household undermine her willingness to be a disciple of Jesus. Herod was responsible for the beheading of John the Baptist and was not on good terms with Jesus, John's cousin. Joanna was among the first to witness Jesus's resurrection, and she reported it to the eleven disciples (Luke 24:9-10). She was wealthy and affluent but humble.

## SUSANNA (Luke 8:2-3)

Susanna also followed Jesus closely and served in his earthly ministry after being cured of a disease or delivered from evil spirits. Her name being mentioned alongside the other female disciples indicates high social standing. However, these women did not let their high-ranking positions stop them from helping spread the gospel message in the way Jesus did by going from city to city.

Susanna was known for her devotion, courage and leadership qualities among the faithful women in the gospel ministry. She also contributed financially to support Jesus's needs and work. She walked with Jesus until his crucifixion, remained at the foot of the cross, then followed on to his grave and eventually witnessed his glorious resurrection (Mark 15:41).

## MARY AND MARTHA (Luke 10:38-42)

Martha and Mary of Bethany were sisters to Lazarus, whom Jesus raised from the dead four days after his burial (John 11:1-45). They ministered in the company of the Lord Jesus and His disciples, in their unique ways of hospitality and love. Martha opened her house to their guests and followed up with all the preparations needed to welcome and entertain them. But Mary sat at Jesus's feet and listened to His teachings. Martha then demanded that Mary come to help her, saying, *'Lord, don't you care that my sister has left me to do the work by myself? Tell her to help me.'* Jesus answered, *'Martha, Martha, you are worried and upset about many things, but only one thing is needed. Mary has chosen what is better, and it will not be taken away from her'* (Luke 10:40-42).

Jesus's answer to Martha was a lesson on getting one's priorities right. Martha got distracted with the practical needs of their guests, which was temporal; whilst Mary dwelt on the spiritual aspects of Jesus's mission, which was eternal (2 Corinthians 4:18).

Mary's affection was set on the Lord Jesus and his eternal kingdom. Her spiritual insight prompted her readiness to act on her faith in Christ as the Lord. *'What good is it for a man to gain the whole world, yet forfeit his soul?'* (Mark 8:36).

Jesus taught and demonstrated the importance of putting God first in all circumstances. He sacrificed Himself to the point of dying on the cross to become the propitiation for the sins of mankind and the whole world (1 John 2:2). Believers are therefore admonished to seek first the kingdom of God and His righteousness, and all other things will be added to them (Matthew 6:33).

## THE WOMAN WITH THE ALABASTER JAR (Matthew 26:6-13; Mark 14:3-9; Luke 7:36-50)

This woman's name is not mentioned in the synoptic gospels, but the Gospel of John distinctively names her as Mary, the sister of Martha and Lazarus of Bethany (John 11:1-2; 12:2-3). Her unexpected but remarkable deed of washing Jesus's feet with her tears, wiping them with her hair, kissing them and pouring expensive perfume on Him, was well noted. Jesus interpreted her acts as preparing His body for His impending death and burial. He reacted to her heart of love, repentance, honour, and sacrifice, along with her faith, with forgiveness and blessings. He pronounced, *'Truly I tell you, wherever this gospel is preached throughout the world, what she has done will also be told, in memory of her'* (Matthew 26:13).

This woman, whom society labelled 'a sinner', was aware of her shortcomings, hence her humble approach to Jesus and the well of tears that streamed down her face. She did not let anything or anyone stop her from discerning the right time to reach out to the Saviour for mercy and breakthrough. She went 'all out' with her most valuable possession to give worship and sacrifice without holding anything back. She must have known that the sacrifices God does not despise are a broken spirit and a contrite heart. Mary's selfless act of giving her best to honour Jesus echoes King David's attitude of not sacrificing to the Lord without a cost. His honest response to Araunah, who offered him a free threshing floor to build an altar for the Lord, was *'No, I insist on paying you for it. I will not sacrifice to the Lord my God burnt offerings that cost me nothing'* (2 Samuel 24:24).

God sees not as man sees. *'Man looks at the outward appearance, but the Lord looks at the heart'* (1 Samuel 16:7).

## THE SAMARITAN WOMAN (John 4:1-42)

On one of His travels from Judea to Galilee, Jesus purposely passed through the Samarian town of Sychar, near Jacob's well, with His disciples. Tired from the journey, He sat by the well to rest while His disciples went into town to buy food. In the afternoon, a Samaritan woman came to draw water from the well. Jesus asked her for a drink, which baffled her because in her society women were considered inferior. Men, especially of Jesus's calibre as a respected rabbi, would avoid speaking to a woman in public. Moreover, Jews and Samaritans did not associate with each other culturally. Jesus disregarded all social barriers and chose a woman as a witness of His Lordship to the Samaritans.

Usually, women living in desert towns would fill their water jars at sunrise and sunset when it would not be too hot to go out. However, this Samaritan woman deliberately chose to go to the well in the afternoon, at the sixth hour of a searing heat under the scorching sun. She carefully planned her trip to the well at a time when she would barely encounter people, but God had a plan to fulfil that day that superseded hers. For *'In his heart a man plans his course, but the LORD determines his steps'* Proverbs 16:9)

Her scorned social status, as the Lord Jesus later revealed during their encounter, caused her to avoid the people in her community. It transpired that she had married five times and was a mistress to the man in her life at that moment.

She was guided by the Spirit of God, at that sun-scorched moment, to meet up with Jesus at the well for a timely encounter that sealed her salvation. Her willingness to engage in open and honest conversation with the Messiah, whose ultimate mission here on earth was to seek and save the lost, enabled her breakthrough. She stumbled into grace and secured her freedom from the dominion of darkness into God's marvellous light (Luke 19:10; Colossians 1:13-14).

Her encounter with Jesus fulfilled God's promise to His children, as spoken through the prophet Isaiah:

> *The LORD will guide you always; he will satisfy your needs in a sun-scorched land and will strengthen your frame. You will be like a well-watered garden, like a spring whose waters never fail.*
> *Isaiah 58:11*

This woman was miraculously rewarded for willingly receiving Jesus's offer of living water – salvation – so that she would not be thirsty again spiritually. Her dried-up cup of a despised life, which none of the five men nor anyone could satisfy, was filled to overflowing with a new beginning of affluence, respect and acceptance in her community. This gave her a fresh start in her powerful gospel ministry. She believed in Jesus as the Messiah and, as scripture has said, *'rivers of living water'* flowed from within her, as the most-heard evangelist of the gospel in her town, to the glory of God (John 7:37-38).

Her choice of fetching water at a different time from everyone else became her divine appointment for Jesus to save one more soul for the kingdom of God. Her salvation encounter spread through the entire town when she left behind her water jar and ran back to town to courageously share her testimony of meeting the Messiah and the Saviour, saying, *'Come, see a man who told me everything I ever did. Could this be the Christ?'* (John 4:29).

Jesus turned her darkness into light and gave her beauty for ashes. Her mess became her message of a life changing source of satisfaction and freedom. Consequently, the people came out of the town to meet with Jesus and heard His teachings.

The town also testified to her message, saying, *'We no longer believe just because of what you said; now we have heard for ourselves, and we know that this man really is the Saviour of the world'* (John 4:42).

## LYDIA (Acts 16:13-15)

Lydia of Thyatira is described as a 'worshipper of God'. She was influential and wealthy with a very successful business selling purple fabric in Philippi, a Roman colony and a leading city of Macedonia on the European continent. The colour purple is associated with affluence, royalty and authority, hence demonstrating the significance of her social standing, wealth and connections. One sabbath day she went to the river's shore, a place of prayer, to worship, and there she met Paul and Silas preaching the gospel. The Lord opened her heart to respond to the salvation message, and she became a believer. She was the first Gentile convert in Europe and was baptised with all her household. Afterwards, she insisted on giving hospitality to Paul and his companions as her act of worship, sacrifice and appreciation for the great gift of salvation.

Lydia lived in a society where women associating with foreign men like Paul and his team were frowned upon. Yet she was open with her involvement with the gospel and the church, and persuaded Paul and Silas to stay in her home, saying, *'If you consider me a believer in the Lord, come and stay in my house.'* Her house became the meeting place of the first European church. She consistently showed kindness and hospitality to the Christians, including Paul and his team.

After Paul and Silas were released from prison, where they had been sent for exorcising a demonic spirit from a slave girl who was hindering their ministry, they went to Lydia's house. There they met with the believers, fellowshipped, and encouraged them once again before they left town (Acts 16:40).

Lydia's faith in the Lord and her act of worship encouraged the spread of the gospel in Europe. She eventually became a leader of the church in Philippi, without letting her career aspirations distract her. She sought the kingdom of God first over her lucrative business.

## PRISCILLA (Acts 18:18-26)

Priscilla was a confident and devoted wife to her husband, Aquila. She was a valued co-worker in the gospel and well-versed in the Word of God. She and Aquila made their living in collaboration with Paul in a tent-making business. One of the churches in Corinth met at their house. Paul described her as 'a fellow worker in Christ' and mentioned that the couple risked their lives for him and all the churches of the Gentiles. They also accompanied Paul on his missionary journey to Ephesus and led the church there. A man named Apollos came to Ephesus and preached in the synagogue. The Bible describes Apollos as *'a learned man with a thorough knowledge of scripture. He spoke with great favour and taught about Jesus accurately.'* However, on hearing his teachings, Priscilla and Aquila invited him to their house and corrected him about Christian doctrine (Acts 18:24-25). They also taught and mentored new believers with biblical knowledge and understanding. After a while in Ephesus, Priscilla and Aquila returned to Rome, as mentioned in Paul's letter to the Romans, where Paul gave special greetings to them and the members of their house church (Romans 16:3-4).

Priscilla and Aquila evidently returned to Ephesus, for the last mention of them was at the very end of Paul's life, when he greeted them in his letter to Timothy (2 Timothy 4:19).

Priscilla dedicated her entire life to Christian ministry, in conjunction with being a wife, as well as pursuing her talent in the tent-making trade. She consciously made a great effort to study scripture and confidently imparted sound Christian doctrine to her followers. She was a respected leader in the early church, hence her name unexpectedly preceding her husband's in Paul's greetings. This may indicate her outstanding contribution to the body of Christ. However, she worked side by side with her husband for mutual support and wider outreach.

## PHOEBE (Romans 16:1-2)

Phoebe, whose name means 'pure' or 'radiant as the moon', was a Greek woman of significance and a Gentile Christian. She was a leader of the church at Cenchreae, a port city near Corinth, where Paul wrote his letters to the Romans. She was entrusted by Paul to deliver his letter to the believers in Rome; he spoke highly of her in the letter and recommended that she be welcomed worthily. He described her as a sister, deacon and benefactor to many, he himself included. She used her wealth and influence to serve her community as a philanthropist and patron. She looked after the interests of others, including the church.

It was not stated whether she herself actually preached to proclaim the gospel to her world, but her lifestyle ministered a profound sermon of God's love, mercy and grace for all. She became a pure and a radiant light of the gospel message of Jesus through her dedication, love, commitment and care for the needy and the vulnerable in her community, including the poor, widows, orphans and the sick; some of whom were cared for in her own house and from her own resources.

## JUNIA (Romans 16:7)

Paul mentioned Junia in his letter to the Romans as a respected and diligent co-worker of the gospel. He also endorsed her, along with Andronicus, as *'outstanding among the apostles'*. She and Andronicus were fellow Jews and relatives of Paul, who were at one stage in prison with him for believing and preaching the gospel of Jesus Christ. In coupling Junia with Andronicus in his greetings, Paul was implying they were either a married couple or brother and sister. Junia was in Christ before Paul's conversion, therefore she had experiential testimonies about witnessing and sharing the good news to motivate and strengthen her fellow Christians, including Paul. She was said to be a female apostle and was noted for her leadership skills.

Junia is an encouragement for steadfastness in keeping the faith in the face of persecution and even imprisonment for the proclamation of the gospel. She also demonstrates that women are as capable as men to serve in the church ministry in any capacity that their calling leads them to, for the edification of the body of Christ, to the honour and glory of God (Ephesians 4:11-12).

## TRYPHENA AND TRYPHOSA (Romans 16:12)

Tryphena and Tryphosa, likely to be sisters or twins, were believed to be of Roman descent, with high social standing and from an upper-class family. Like some of the female disciples of Jesus, they set aside the luxurious lives their names imply ('dainty', 'elegant', 'luxurious'). They worked hard with all their hearts to promote the gospel message, with phenomenal devotion and love for the Lord and for their fellow believers. The apostle Paul commended them for their efforts in promoting the kingdom of the Lord.

## PERSIS (Romans 16:12)

Persis was another dear friend of Paul, and a fellow worker in the gospel ministry whom he described as the *'beloved who laboured hard in the Lord'*. Her name implies she was a Persian, and she might have been brought to Rome as a slave.

Yet, Tryphena and Tryphosa did not look down on her but worked alongside her in peaceful collaboration of spirit and of love and respect. The two sisters acted by the very word of the gospel message that *'There is neither Jew nor Gentile, neither slave nor free, nor is there male and female, for you are all one in Christ Jesus'* (Galatians 3:28-29).

## EUODIA AND SYNTYCHE (Philippians 4:2-3)

Euodia and Syntyche were leaders involved in building the church in Philippi around 61AD. Paul commended them in his letter to the Church as being 'labourers' and 'contenders' at his side in the common goal of spreading the gospel. They devoted themselves to promote the message of the cross with him, despite their disagreements with each other. Paul, however, pleaded with them to unite and be of one mind in sharing the gospel of peace for which they had been called.

Euodia and Syntyche's disagreement, and Paul's plea for them to be of one mind in their quest for salvation, teaches that the body of Christ works better together when united in love and harmony. Unity is power, and two are known to be better than one because they have a good return for their labour (Ecclesiastes 4:9).

The Master, Jesus Christ Himself, spoke to His disciples through a parable about the importance of unity and the benefits of Christian fellowship. When He was accused by the Pharisees of healing a demon-possessed man by the power of Beelzebub, the Prince of demons, His response was, '*Every kingdom divided against itself will be ruined, and every city or household that is divided against itself cannot stand*' (Matthew 12:24-26, Mark 3:25-26).

God desires that His children work together in one accord, and in love to reflect His glory. Therefore, as Jesus Christ was about to leave the earth, He prayed to God the Father to protect His disciples and all believers by the power of His name so that they may be one, as He and the Father are one, as a testimony to the world (John 17:11-12; 20-21).

Paul consistently opposed and discouraged discord and disunity in the early churches. He often cautioned them in his teachings and writings to unite in all aspects and circumstances for the well-being of the entire congregation. He taught that all disagreements are strategies of Satan to derail soul-winning for God's kingdom (see Amos 3:3; 1Corinthians 1:10; Philippians 1:27).

Paul had a two-way approach in reconciling Euodia and Syntyche, as a peace-precedent and lasting solution for the church. First, he pleaded with the women to avoid unnecessary disputes that were *'unprofitable'* and to *'be of the same mind'*. They were to *'do nothing out of selfish ambition or vain conceit, but in humility consider others better than themselves.'* They were to look not only to their own interests, *'but also to the interests of others'* (Philippians 2:3-4). Secondly, Paul made an urgent plea to the other leaders in the church to help Euodia and Syntyche reconcile and return to being like-minded, one in spirit and of one mind in the Lord (Philippians 4:3). This required prayer and the Word of God, for:

> *All Scripture is God-breathed and is useful for teaching, rebuking, correcting and training in righteousness, so that the servant of God may be thoroughly equipped for every good work.*
> *2 Timothy 3:16-17*

Euodia and Syntyche's story, therefore, teaches that conflict is inevitable in personal relationships; hence, it is humanly impossible to live in total harmony with people at all times. Paul himself was no stranger to conflict – he disagreed with Barnabas over John Mark during their missionary work (Acts 15:36-40).

God knows our human weaknesses and imperfections; therefore, He sent His Son to show believers how to resolve conflicts and settle disagreements among themselves. Jesus taught His disciples about conflict resolution, the believers-way, in Matthew 18:15-17. Here believers are taught to face the conflict and deal with it then forgive the conflict and move ahead in harmony, as Euodia and Syntyche were encouraged to do. After some time, Paul found a place in his heart to resolve his grudge against John Mark by inviting him to come along and minister with him (2 Timothy 4:9-11).

Unity is a bedrock for peaceful, blessed and successful living. The Psalmist sums it up so beautifully:

> *How good and pleasant it is when brethren live together in unity! It is like precious oil poured on the head, running down the beard, running down on Aaron's beard, down on the collar of his robe. It is as if the dew of Hermon were falling on Mount Zion. For there the Lord bestows His blessing, even life forevermore.*
> *Psalm 133*

## LOIS AND EUNICE (2 Timothy 1:5)

Lois and Eunice were Timothy's grandmother and mother respectively. Eunice was a Jewish believer but married to a Greek Gentile husband (Acts 16:1,3). However, she raised their son Timothy to be thoroughly conversant with the Jewish religion, a foundation laid by her own mother Lois for her to build on by faith. Paul recognised that fundamental knowledge and understanding of the holy scriptures in Timothy and openly praised Lois and Eunice for training the boy in a godly manner.

Timothy's godly upbringing made him wise for salvation through faith in Christ and also aided his spiritual acceleration to become a leader of the church in Ephesus (2 Timothy 3:15). Lois and Eunice are role models for consistency in faith and an uncompromising attitude in raising godly children.

## APPHIA (Philemon 1:1-25)

Apphia, who was described by Paul as 'our sister' in his letter to Philemon, is believed to be Philemon's wife. The couple offered their home as a church for their fellow Christians for meetings and sharing the love of Jesus. Paul appreciated their faith in Christ and their love for all the saints with great joy, encouragement and thanksgiving to the Lord, as stated in his letter. He also appealed to the family to receive their runaway slave Onesimus back as a fellow saint and a dear brother in Christ, exactly as they would Paul himself. This was in fulfilment of Galatians 3:25-29. In addition, he pledged to reimburse any debt that Onesimus owed to Philemon.

All these dedicated female adherents of the gospel mentioned, and many more whose passion were unnoticed by human eyes, pursued religious liberty through their experiential knowledge and understanding of the work of the cross. The conviction of their new life of liberty, through their faith in Christ, made many of them renounce their old religious practices of Judaism and other faiths without any fear of persecution, prosecution or death. Their new way of life in Christ constantly attracted controversies and conflicts. However, knowing they were not contending with flesh and blood but against spiritual forces of the evil principalities of this dark world, they remained steadfast in faith. They also devoted themselves to constant prayers with fasting for the resolve of their challenges. Some of the solutions to their prayer needs were instantaneous and miraculously accomplished, but some of the women suffered martyrdom and others had to wait on God longer for resolutions, as testing of their faith (see Luke 2:36-38; Acts 12:5; Ephesians 6:12).

They were relationally committed and connected with their worship, authentic fellowship and their active serving of one another. They financially gave to support, maintain and sustain 'The Way' movement, as the early Jewish Christians called the church (Acts 24:14).

Their benevolence continued to benefit the missionary works of the disciples after the death and ascension of the Lord Jesus Christ. They affectionately embraced, encouraged and cared for the vulnerable and the marginalised in their midst.

They practiced hospitality, led the constant meal-sharing practice of the church, shared their possessions and proceeds from land or house sales to help the poor, and ensured that there were no needy persons among them (Acts 2:44-46; 4:32-35).

They were zealous and passionate enough to effect changes to the concept of gender discrimination in religious practices. Some women believers consistently met up with the apostles in the temple courts to receive biblical wisdom, knowledge and understanding, which equipped and empowered them to spread the gospel.

Most of the women offered their homes for fellowship and consequently became house church leaders through the grace upon them. They praised God, broke bread and enjoyed the favour of all the people with gladness and sincere hearts. There was evidence of miraculous signs following their prayers, confessions and testimonies of the resurrected Christ (Acts 1:14; 12:5-17).

Their selfless acts of service alongside the disciples fulfilled God's divine purpose of creating the woman as a suitable helpmeet for man (Genesis 2:18 – God's gracious gift to man). Their deeds were undeniably evident in their lives. They were the kind of Christians that the apostle Paul would describe as 'living epistles known and read of all men' (2 Corinthians 3:3).

With the enabling of the Holy Spirit, some women like Priscilla, Phoebe, Mary and Junia soared beyond the boundaries of household and community meetings and travelled into other villages, towns and cities to plant churches with Paul (Romans 12:1-21; Revelation 12:11).

# THE MINISTRY OF PHBC WOMEN

The acts of love, mutual fellowship and sacrificial service demonstrated by the women of the early Christian church have also been the essential practice of most women in the church I have attended for the past 25 years. I personally served as a member of the intercessory prayer team and occasionally led worship. Pollards Hill Baptist Church (PHBC) in South London, whose mission statement is *'Sharing the love of Jesus'*, is blessed with women actively involved in administration, organisation of church activities, leading worship, home-cell groups and lay preaching.

In the cell groups, participants discuss and share their thoughts and concerns alongside the Sunday sermon scriptures. The cell group study materials are designed to inform and entreat participants to engage and seek understanding of the scriptures. Members are encouraged to get involved with church activities, which enable them to discover, develop and share their God-given gifts and talents with the church family, the community and their world.

They are motivated to take an interest in church meetings together for the promotion of their spiritual growth and the confidence to know they are not walking the Christian journey alone (see Matthew 18:20; Hebrews 10:25).

The ministry of the church's quarterly prayer walks in the community is led by a faithful female member. Beginning with prayer in the church hall, each prayer walker is given a set of prayer points carefully put together for the needs of the community. Walkers first gather in the sanctuary on the designated day, to pray for God's mercy and leading as they journey through the community. Prayers are raised for residents, businesses, churches, schools, and all activities that take place in the community. Often there are opportunities to witness, as people want to know why the church is out there praying.

Another team of dedicated women in the church give their time to serve and share the love of Jesus with parents, carers and their young children. This friendly group was started in 1978 by Noreen Want, a faithful member of the church. Noreen was assisted by Joan Winrow, now the oldest member of the church at 97, to welcome mothers with little children who needed a respite over a coffee break away from home. Some men attended too, coming along after dropping their children in the local schools around the church. This act of kindness eventually turned into the formal 'Tots & Tinies' meetings, centred around play, learning, sharing and growing with biblical principles. It is a way to *'train a child in the way he should go, and when he is old he will not turn from it* (Proverbs 22:6) and to spread the gospel of love as a reflection of God (1 Corinthians 13:13).

Another female member of the church, Pastor Stella Aryiku, organises the Hope Coffee Club for the over 55s. Stella felt called to rise above her widowhood to minister God's salvation message and to extend acts of love, hope and hospitality to the lonely and vulnerable elderly in the community. She hosts senior citizens in general and also from the local nursing home for weekly coffee meetings. Participants socialise and draw comfort from one another over refreshments and conversations.

Various activities are offered throughout the month including physical fitness, storytelling, quizzes and a special Wednesday reflection known as the 'God stop' where Stella shares the love of Jesus through the Word of God and gospel songs. Throughout the year, members enjoy an annual delectable Easter buffet, Summer BBQs and Christmas parties, which foster a sense of value, joy, neighbourly connections and stronger bonds of friendship. Pastor Stella could not have supported and entertained the senior citizens without the dedication and consistent commitment of other church members, namely Mary Wrey, Cathy Johnson, Mary Asare and Edward Gyenning.

# THE PURPOSE OF A WOMAN'S MINISTRY

*All authority in heaven and on earth has been given to me. Therefore, GO and MAKE DISCIPLES of all nations, baptising them in the name of the Father and of the Son and of the Holy Spirit, and teaching them to obey everything that I have commanded you. And surely I am with you always, to the very end of the age.*
*Matthew 28:18-20*

In His divine plan, God thought it was not good for a man to be alone, so He made him a suitable helper. He caused Adam to fall into a deep sleep, and while he was sleeping, He took one of his ribs and closed up the place with flesh. He subsequently made a woman from the rib and gave her to Adam as his companion and wife. Adam was grateful to God for his helpmeet: *'This is now bone of my bones and flesh of my flesh; she shall be called 'woman' for she was taken out of man'* (Genesis 2:23).

Adam and Eve became God's initial workmanship, created in His image for companionship and relationship with Him and others and for the good works He prepared in advance for mankind (Genesis 2:18-24).

Jesus Christ fulfilled God's divine plan by including women in His earthly ministry, as partakers of God's divine inheritance. He walked and worked with women until his death on the cross. He defied the indelible tradition of women being segregated in society and approved of them by constantly breaking social barriers and defending them with open arms, compassion and love. He publicly acknowledged and commended women for their courage, zeal and consistent commitment to their services as co-workers of God's kingdom. He elevated, valued, befriended, healed, protected, and comforted women. He also encouraged, motivated and empowered them to confidently use their spiritual gifts and talents to help spread the gospel.

Jesus mostly showcased women as vessels of active faith and models of God's glory, whom we have already considered. Additional examples include:

i. The woman with the issue of bleeding for twelve years was instantly healed when she touched the fringe of Jesus's cloak. She said to herself, *'If I only touch his cloak, I will be healed.'* Jesus, feeling the impact of the power that had gone out of Him, turned and demanded to know who touched Him. The trembling woman fell at His feet as a response, but He reassured her, saying, *'Daughter, your faith has healed you. Go in peace'* (Matthew 9:20-22, Luke 8:43-48).

ii. The Syro-Phoenician woman demonstrated great faith prior to the healing of her demon-possessed daughter. When she approached Jesus with her request, she was immediately reminded of her social standing as a second-class citizen in the land who had no priority in anything. But instead of being discouraged by Jesus's unpleasant but honest response that it was *'not right to take the children's bread and throw it to their dogs',* she patiently and humbly accepted her stigmatised social status and settled for the crumbs that fell from the children's table. Jesus found her response astonishing and, as a result, healed her daughter for her incredible and great faith (Matthew 15:21-28, Mark 7:24-30).

iii. Jesus healed a woman crippled with a spirit of infirmity and bent over for eighteen years – on a Sabbath day. Jesus was teaching in one of the synagogues when He saw the bent-over woman, faithfully attending service to hear the word of God. Letting nothing or no one be in the way of His compassion and love, He called her forward and said to her, *'Woman, you are set free from your infirmity.'*

After this pronouncement, He put His hands on her, and immediately she straightened up and praised God with joyful thanks for setting her free from bondage, taking away her shame and honouring her as a true daughter of Abraham, thus qualifying her *'to share in the inheritance of the saints'* in the kingdom of light (Luke 13:10-17; Colossians 1:12).

# CHRISTIAN WOMEN IN FAITH FROM HISTORY TO THE PRESENT DAY

In addition to the outstanding contributions of all the women from the biblical narratives, the following Christian women of faith also rendered remarkable services to society. They led in the running of schools for girls to offer basic education, established healthcare training for women, instituted orphanages, developed shelters for the ostracised, and offered vocation for the poor and the homeless. These heroines of faith presented themselves to God and his will as women who did not need to be ashamed of their beliefs. They allowed their inner lights to shine before men and to the world, despite the ongoing societal oppositions to female leadership (2 Timothy 2:15).

## SUSANNA WESLEY (1669-1742)

Susanna Wesley was an accomplished writer, theologian and teacher, who strongly believed that girls should be educated in the same capacity as boys. She home-schooled all ten of her children and was known for her astute household discipline and organisational skills.

In the midst of her very busy life as a wife and mother to ten surviving children out of nineteen births, Susanna successfully managed a consistent two-hour daily prayer routine, with intercessions and personal Bible study. She was able to make this possible by retreating to a designated place of privacy in the house and covering her head with her kitchen apron; a signal to her children and every other person in her household to respect her prayer time with no distractions or disturbances.

Susanna's daily dwelling in God's presence – the 'secret place' that she consciously created as her act of worship and service – helped build her own faith and that of her family. As a result, two of her sons, John and Charles Wesley, became great evangelists of the Methodist church in England and abroad. This earned Susanna the title 'Mother of Methodism'.

Susanna also organised Sunday afternoon Bible teaching meetings in her kitchen with some church members and other people from her community. Word quickly circulated about her immense knowledge of the Bible and how well she communicated its truths. The numbers attending her informal Sunday afternoon Bible study grew so much that, on a given Sunday after church, Susanna would have as many as two hundred people in attendance, meaning she had to move her meetings to a larger venue.

Furthermore, Susanna masterminded the 'lay preaching' concept in the Methodist church, as she appointed people who were knowledgeable in the Bible and spirit-filled to preach when her husband, the resident pastor of the church, was not around to take the service.

## ELIZABETH FRY (1780-1845)

Elizabeth Fry (nee Gurney) was born in Norwich into the influential Quaker family that played a pivotal part in establishing the Gurney's Bank in 1770 (this eventually merged into Barclays Bank). She was married to Joseph Fry, a fellow Quaker and a tea merchant, and the couple moved to London. They were blessed with 11 children, who were all raised in Joseph's family home of Plashet House in East Ham, before moving to Ramsgate.

In 1813, Elizabeth visited Newgate Prison and was taken aback by the appalling conditions that women were subjected to. Women and their children were kept in 'dark, dirty and dangerous' environments. Her religious beliefs and compassion for the sick, poor and lonely, coupled with her heart for the ostracised in society, motivated her passion for her prison ministry. She believed that every prisoner should be reformed, not just punished.

She put her words into action by unreservedly contributing to teaching the female prisoners and their children skills like literacy and Bible reading, as well as knitting and sewing to earn a living. She also instructed inmates on mercy instead of judgment from the chapel she established in the prison. She believed every human being has the ability to change through the power of God's word. She was quoted as being careful not to say, *'I am more holy than thou,'* but instead *'to keep in perpetual remembrance that all have sinned and come short of the glory of God'* (Romans 3:23).

She established the British Ladies' Society for Promoting the Reformation of Female Prisoners in 1817, with branches in Russia, Switzerland, Italy and the Netherlands. She also helped improve prison conditions on convict ships, which resulted in the production of the Rajah Quilt, which to this day is on display in the National Gallery of Australia. Her campaign for prison reforms was eventually passed in Parliament as a legislation in 1823. She was nicknamed 'The Angel of Prisons'.

In addition to being a prison reformer, she was an advocate for mental health, an abolitionist, philanthropist, and preacher. She was officially recognised as a Quaker Minister of the Religious Society of Friends in 1811. She conducted Sunday School in her house for local children and taught them to read and write with sound biblical knowledge and as a way of life.

She opened homeless shelters, including a refuge for prostitutes in Hackney. She set up soup kitchens and fed the poor. She helped with the distribution of smallpox inoculations for children in the East Ham community. In co-founding schools for girls, she established The Institution of Nursing School in 1840, where nursing standards were highly improved. Her nurses were instructed to treat both the poor and the wealthy in the same way. Some nurses from her training school worked in the Crimean War under Florence Nightingale, who was influenced by Elizabeth's work.

Her involvement in campaigning for the abolition of the slave trade prompted her to write in her diary: *'At the close of this year, in public matters, I looked upon slavery being abolished as an unspeakable blessing.'* Elizabeth was also the face of the old five-pound notes between 2000 and 2016. Queen Victoria, who took an interest in Elizabeth Fry's work and financially supported it, described her as a 'very superior person'. Her legacy of prison reform, literacy and vocations for women, as well as her support for the poor, the vulnerable, and the mentally unstable, were built on the solid rock of her faith in God.

## ELIZABETH CADY-STANTON (1815-1902)

Elizabeth was a well-known women's advocate and a campaigner for gender equality, stating that: *'We hold these truths to be self-evident: that all men and women were created equal.'* Her dream of going to college did not materialise, because no colleges accepted female students at that time. She worked tirelessly to liberate women from being labelled as society's second best. She also campaigned for women to be given the right to education, property and the right to vote through the Declaration of Sentiments at the Seneca Falls Convention.

Having seven children who needed her full attention at home meant that Elizabeth needed assistance to accomplish her mission as an activist and abolitionist, and her friend Susan Anthony became a perfect partner. Susan coordinated affairs perfectly in the background while Elizabeth wrote. Susan delivered the speeches, circulated petitions and secured the halls for their meetings. Elizabeth herself said, *'I forged the thunderbolts, she fired them.'*

Together, they achieved a great deal of social liberties, inclusion and respect for women. On the dedication page of her *Eighty Years and More* memoirs, Elizabeth said, *'I dedicate this volume to Susan B. Anthony, my steadfast friend for half a century.'* Elizabeth died in 1902, 18 years before women achieved the right to vote in the United States via the 19th amendment, which became law in 1920. Her house is now a part of the Women's Rights National Historical Park in Seneca Falls, New York.

## FLORENCE NIGHTINGALE (1820-1910)

Florence Nightingale was born in Florence and baptised in the Church of England by her Christian parents. Her decision at the age of 16 to become a nurse was strongly opposed by her parents, who deemed nursing unsuitable for a well-educated woman. But Florence stood firm and maintained her conviction of being called by God into nursing care. She did not give up but waited patiently for God's appointed time (Habakkuk 2:3). Her father eventually agreed for her to pursue her passion of nursing as her career choice. She went ahead to train in Germany to become a qualified nurse.

The wonderful works of Florence's calling became most evident during her immense contribution to nursing the wounded soldiers in the Crimean War between Great Britain and Russia. She worked tirelessly to give a high standard of care to patients in the Barrack Hospital at Scutari in Turkey. Her paramount priority was to achieve cleaner hospital environments for both patients and their caregivers, for safe and positive care outcomes. One of her numerous famous quotes was: *'Every nurse ought to be careful to wash her hands very frequently during the day. If her face too, so much better.'*

Dedicated and caring, Florence would consistently check on the well-being of the wounded soldiers. She tended to walk through the dark hallways of the hospital at night, carrying out her ward rounds with a lamp. This resulted in her nicknames: 'The Lady with the Lamp' and 'The Angel of Crimea'. That light she carried symbolised life, hope and comfort for the suffering. Florence Nightingale publicly spoke about her desire for nursing as a calling from God. She understood that *'Religion is not devotion, but work and suffering for the love of God...'* Apparently, in a conversation with one of her night-nurse colleagues, she referred to the answer that the Virgin Mary gave to the angel Gabriel at the annunciation of Jesus's birth, saying, *"Behold the handmaid of the Lord'* (see Luke 1:26-38), *and so have I said in my youth; may we all answer the angel as Mary did.'*

When the war ended, Queen Victoria presented Florence with a specially designed diamond brooch with the inscription 'To Miss Florence Nightingale, as a mark of esteem and gratitude for her devotion toward the Queen's brave soldiers, from Victoria R. 1855'.

Florence also established St. Thomas's Hospital in London as well as the Nightingale Training School for Nurses in 1860, for quality patient care. Her healthcare expertise reduced hospital deaths by two thirds in the Crimean era. Her successful endeavour in nursing raised the standard and the reputation of healthcare. This motivated young women to follow in her footsteps, and thus she became known as the founder of modern nursing. All her actions, reports and recommendations concerning better healthcare were evidence-based and credible.

Florence contracted 'Crimean fever' at the age of 38, which rendered her housebound and bedridden for 11 years. However, as determined in her faith and dedicated to work as she was, Florence continued discharging her healthcare duties from her bed at home. She was frequently consulted about field hospital management and public sanitation throughout the American civil war. She also had a big influence on Indian nursing. She continued to work until she died at the age of 90. Her birthday on May 12th is annually celebrated as International Nurses' Day, in honour of her memory.

## FANNY CROSBY (1820-1915)

Frances Jane Crosby, who became well known as Fanny Crosby, was born in March 1820. At six weeks old, she lost her sight to an eye infection and medical negligence. When she was six months old, her father passed away after contracting pneumonia. Her grandmother helped with her upbringing so that her mother could go to work. Fanny recalled her grandmother Eunice praying, reciting poetry and reading the Bible to her every day, with unending reassurances that God had a special purpose for everything He made, and that included her. At age eight, she made up a poem and recited it to her grandmother:

*Oh, what a happy child I am,*
*Although I cannot see!*
*I am resolved that in this world.*
*Contented I will be!*
*How many blessings I enjoy*
*That other people don't!*
*To weep or sigh because I'm blind,*
*I cannot and I won't.*

Her grandmother also helped her to memorise parts of the Bible, and by the time she was 12 years old, she had memorised verses from Genesis, Exodus, Leviticus, Numbers, Psalms and also from all the four gospels. In her own words, the Bible verses were like friends that cheered her up whenever she felt sad about not going to school. At 15, her prayers for being in school were answered when she was admitted to the New York Institution for the Blind (NYIB). Whilst there, a visiting Scottish phrenologist examined her work and proclaimed her a poet. She wrote poems for presidents and governors and read them out when they visited her school.

She also learnt to play the harp and the piano, which enabled her to play most of her poems as songs and hymns. After her graduation from the NYIB, at the age of 22, she was employed as a teacher there.

Fanny married Alexander Van Alstyne, her long-time friend, who was also blind and a fellow teacher in NYIB. He was a gifted musical composer and exceptional organist. He helped her with most of her compositions. Fanny wrote more than 9,000 songs in her lifetime, including *Pass Me Not, O Gentle Saviour, Rescue the Perishing, To God be the Glory,* and *Blessed Assurance.* In the latter, Fanny amazingly describes 'visions of rapture' bursting on her sight – *'angels descending, bring from above, echoes of mercy, whispers of love'.* It was her faith in God that inspired her to write her poems and songs.

She was the first woman to ever address the American Senate and Congress at Capitol Hill. Her speech aided the exposure and recognition of the blind and the disabled in society. She also travelled to different cities to speak about her faith in Jesus, and often dismissed sympathetic attitudes towards her by saying, *'Don't waste sympathy on me; I am the happiest person alive.'*

Fanny Crosby led a God-loving and faith-filled life of contentment, humility, compassion and generosity. She fulfilled Jesus's word in Matthew 10:8: *'Freely ye have received, freely give.'* She willingly gave to the needy out of the proceeds from her songs and poetry. She died at 94 years.

## CHARLOTTE 'LOTTIE' MOON (1840-1912)

Charlotte Moon was a Southern Baptist missionary. She ministered in China for forty years as a teacher and evangelist with the Foreign Mission Board. She established girls' schools and propagated the biblical great commission by preaching the gospel in various Chinese villages. She also helped to improve the working conditions of other missionaries. The Baptist Women's Missionary Union still collects the 'Lottie Moon Christmas Offering' every year in her memory. This money is used to support international missions.

## MARY MITCHELL SLESSOR (1848-1915)

Mary Slessor was born in Gilcomston, Aberdeen in Scotland, on December 2, 1848, to Robert and Mary Slessor. She was the second of seven children and is described as one of the most outstanding missionaries in the history of the church. Her family's financial hardship, due to her father's alcoholism, which disrupted his trade as a shoemaker, forced Mary to work in the Baxter Brothers' Mill at the age of eleven.

She started as a part-timer and attended school alongside her work. By 14, she had become skilled and was working up to 12 hours a day in the mill in order to help pay the household bills and put food on the table.

Mary's mother was a devout Christian and attended the United Free Presbyterian Wishart Church with her children. Mary accepted Jesus Christ as her personal Saviour in her teens, and with her approachable, caring and empathetic nature, became a Sunday School teacher (volunteering). Mary, who passionately evangelised to her students and wholeheartedly cared for the underprivileged children of her community, also had to deal cautiously and tenaciously with undisciplined gangs who infested her neighbourhood and regularly threatened the mission teachers. Despite the stronger men in the church being protective of the vulnerable teachers and escorting them from the danger zone every Sunday, Mary fell prey to a street gang one Sunday night. The callous leader of the gang carried a leaden weight at the end of a cord and swung it round Mary's head until it came close enough to touch her brow. But she did not blanch. The weight crashed to the ground and the leader exclaimed, 'She's game, boys!' Subsequently, the gang went along with her to her meeting. The enemy intended to harm her, *'but God intended it for good to accomplish the saving of many lives'* (Genesis 50:20). On the wall of one of her hut houses in West Africa hung a picture of that gang leader with his wife and family. They became family friends.

Through her mother's influence and keenness on missionaries, Mary got access to the monthly *Missionary Record*, a magazine published by the Presbyterian Church to inform members of missionary needs and activities. Mary idolised David Livingstone, the famous missionary and explorer, and she decided to follow his footsteps and become a missionary, especially when her brother John could not fulfil their mother's desire of him becoming a missionary due to ill health and death. At about 27 years of age, she applied to train at the Foreign Mission Board of the United Presbyterian Church in Edinburgh.

After her training in 1876 at age 28, Mary, intentionally ready for the mission with a mindset of *'here am I; send me'*, set sail on the SS Ethiopia for Duke Town in Calabar, in the West African country of Nigeria. As she waited to embark on the steamer, she noticed a large number of casks of spirits being carried on board. That brought to memory her family's ordeal with her father's alcoholism, and she exclaimed, *'Scores of casks and only one missionary!'*

On her arrival in Duke Town, she began serving in the mission's compound dispensary then went on to teach in a day school on the Mission Hill, before making a tour of the stations. Her work involved long and tedious journeys through the bush and along rivers with grave dangers, unpleasant encounters and sometimes death threats from the natives.

Her biggest challenge was sharing the gospel of grace, mercy and peace with people who were divided on cultural differences, sceptical about missionaries and deeply superstitious about women giving birth to twins. Mary boldly assumed an attitude of '*I can do all things through Christ who gives me strength*' and worked above and beyond evangelism. Her own prayer to God was, *'Lord, the task is impossible for me but not for Thee. Lead the way and I will follow. Why should I fear? I am on a Royal Mission. I am in the service of the King of kings.'* With such audacious faith in the Lord, she fearlessly fought hard both physically (with constructive dialogue) and spiritually (by prayer, petitions and supplications) to successfully perform her task of inviting the leading natives to attend church services and to share the gospel openly with the natives. She also provided healthcare services, offered practical vocational training, advocated for women's rights and opposed human trafficking and slavery. In 1895, she founded the Hope Waddell Institute for medical training.

Mary willingly and confidently adapted to the culture of the natives in Calabar by learning their Efik language, understanding their traditional beliefs and empathising with their needs. Mary truly practised what she preached, as scripture says that *'whoever wants to become great among you must be your servant, and whosoever wants to be first must be your slave – just as the Son of Man did not come to be served, but to serve, and to give His life as a ransom for many'* (Matthew 20:26-28).

Her humble approach and her caring attitude towards the people that she ministered to earned her trust and acceptance from the locals and their tribal chiefs. She was nicknamed 'mother of all the people' and was appointed the first female British vice-consul for that area. With her strong personality and faith in the Lord, she was able to rescue and care for numerous women and children affected by tribal wars. She also acted as childminder for hundreds of unwanted children. The natives of Calabar had a belief that one of every twin is a child of an evil spirit, a superstition sadly shared by the twin mothers themselves. Since they could not decide which twin was of the evil spirit, both were taken to a solitary part of the jungle and left to the mercy of beasts and scavengers. The twin mothers were also sent away into the bush and told to never come back home. They either died of starvation or were devoured by wild beasts. Mary rescued and adopted numerous children who had been abandoned to die. She fought hard and long to have that superstitious custom of killing twin babies declared unlawful by the local chiefs.

Mary contracted malaria three years into her first assignment and was brought back to Scotland, where she recovered and then returned to Calabar to continue her ministry. An inspector of missions with the Presbyterian Missions Board was impressed with her dedication and love for the people. Again, three years into her second assignment, at age 34, she was ordered back home with a serious health issue; she stayed longer this time to fully recover. In the course of her recovery, she cared for her ill younger sister, Janie, and eventually her mother, who also fell ill and needed care. With the help of a loyal factory friend who volunteered to look after her sick relatives, Mary was able to return to her mission after she fully recovered. Sadly, she lost both her mother and her sister within a year of returning to work. In her grief, she recalled her mother's response to her missionary journey: *'You are my child, given to me by God, and I have given you back to Him. When He needs you, and where He sends you, there I would have you to be.'*

At this stage, Mary felt led to move from Calabar to Okoyong, an un-evangelised territory, where the occupants were terribly feared. After a period of reluctance at Mary's proposal, the Foreign Mission Committee eventually gave her the permission to go, based on her mission ability and experience with the Calabar natives. She wrote a letter home about her new mission field: *'I am going to a new tribe up-country, a fierce, cruel people, and everyone tells me that they will kill me.'*

King Eyo of Calabar lent her his state canoe to make that all-important journey to begin her new mission at Okoyong. She was welcomed more warmly than she had expected. She held family worship with the crew of the canoe gathered around her before she retired to bed on her first day.

Mary boldly ministered with an ingrained attitude of love, devotion, empathy and compassion toward the natives. She visited the sick, cared for children, encouraged women, comforted the sorrowful and embraced the lonely. She brought scripture to life by becoming the *hands* and *feet* of Christ. She selflessly and wholeheartedly served the community, in God's name and power (see Matthew 25:40).

Mary celebrated a peaceful 15 years of successful integration and acceptance in Okoyong with a grand church service, conducting communion for the first time. The church hall was filled to overflowing. 11 youngsters, some of whom she had rescued, publicly accepted Jesus as their personal Saviour and joined the church. Mary's 'yes' to God's call to minister in Okoyong broke the old heathen order among its inhabitants. Life in the community became safer for all, women were free, slaves enjoyed their rights, trade and industries were established, educational facilities were built for both the young and the old, people openly led the Christian life, and most youths were actively engaged in church activities. Peace reigned, to the glory of God.

Mary prayed for everything and about everything, even the mundane. She was once discovered making cement and when asked whether she'd ever had cement lessons, she said, '*No, I just stir it like porridge, turn it out, smooth it with a stick and all the time keep praying; Lord, here's the cement, if to thy glory set it, and it has never gone once wrong.*' (See Mark 11:23.)

Mary's humility, good humour, patience, quiet demeanour and godly wisdom accorded her respect and an informal position as an arbitrator in Okoyong. She counselled, listened and settled disputes of all kinds, including tribal misunderstandings, pronouncing justice to the ones wrongly accused. Her good works were recognised, and she was made Vice-Consul of Okoyong by Sir Claude MacDonald, the British Consul General of the Niger Coast Protectorate. The governor-general of Northern and Southern Nigeria, Sir Frederick Lugard, also heard about Mary's outstanding contributions to humanity in her missions and recommended that the secretary of state for the colonies bring it to royal notice. At a grand gathering in the Goldie Memorial Hall of Duke Town, Mary was honoured with the Silver Cross of the Order of St. John of Jerusalem in England. On receiving the award, she said, *'Who am I that I should have this? If I have done anything in my life, it has been easy because the Master has gone before.'*

In her frailty at sixty-six, Mary continued reaching out to the lost, looking after orphans and widows and keeping herself from being polluted by the world, until she could no longer move her physical body. She chose her calling of taking the gospel to the remote parts of the world over the comfort of being home in Scotland to minister in church buildings, and she gave herself fully to the work of the Lord.

As described by the apostle Paul, concerning his own life, Mary Slessor, the passionate missionary, made it her goal to please God: She *'fought the good fight, finished the race and kept the faith'.* She peacefully went to be with the Lord on the morning of January 13th 1915, as her five children sat around her bed. She was laid to rest in Duke Town with a great crowd of mourners including government officials, merchants and missionaries.

## EVANGELINE CORY BOOTH (1865-1950)

The formation of the Salvation Army by William and Catherine Booth motivated many Christian women to exhibit their God-given gifts and talents by preaching the gospel in public, teaching in schools, managing orphanages and heading other significant organisations. Evangeline Cory Booth, the daughter of William and Catherine Booth, became the Salvation Army's first female general in 1934, after leading as commander of the American Salvation Army for 30 years.

She began to preach at 15 and headed the Army's International Training College at age 26. She was known to have a strong personality and was described as eloquent with good organisational skills. She was tactful and charming in her approach to minister the Word of God to humanity. She also wrote many hymns for the Salvation Army, with *The World for God* perhaps her most famous.

Her problem-solving skills were manifested through her outstanding services to society. These included: establishing hospitals for unwed mothers, emergency shelters for the homeless, homes for the elderly, soup kitchens for the hungry and the unemployed, and the feeding of 30,000 people one Christmas Day in New York. This benevolence awarded her the Distinguished Service Medal in 1919.

## HENRIETTA MEARS (1890-1963)

Dr Henrietta Cornelia Mears was a Christian educator, author and evangelist. She was born on 23rd October 1890 in Fargo,

North Dakota, as a seventh child to Mr Ashley Mears, owner of more than 20 banks located in the Dakotas, and Margaret Everts Mears, a Baptist laywoman with great spiritual depths, whose father was a prominent pastor in the First Baptist Church of Chicago.

Henrietta declared herself a Christian at age seven, one Easter Sunday morning, and joined the First Baptist Church of Minneapolis. She was baptised soon afterwards. She taught her first class of new Christians at the age of 11, thus foretelling her future ministry. At 12, she contracted muscular rheumatism, which crippled her and left her in constant pain for two years, but she received a miraculous full healing through the prayer of a friend.

She went through elementary school with very poor eyesight that doctors predicted would lead to total blindness by age 30. She was therefore advised against her enrolment into university for further studies, in order to prolong her ability to see. She vehemently rejected that advice, saying, *'Then blind I shall be, but I want something in my head to think about.'* True to her word, and by her unwavering faith in God, she enrolled at the University of Minnesota and graduated with good grades. Whilst a freshman, she served as the superintendent of a Sunday School junior department, and during her senior year she taught a popular women's Bible class at the university. She claimed her failing eyesight had been her greatest spiritual asset and had kept her completely dependent on God.

Her mother passed away when she was 20 years of age. As she grieved her loss, she pondered the words 'spiritual mantle', which her pastor mentioned at the funeral service. She knew that her mother had passed her spiritual influence on to her. This shifted her perspective to seeking more of God to enable her to assume that spiritual responsibility as a perpetual memorial to her mother and as an honour to God. This wholehearted commitment formed the basis of her future ministry.

Moving to Minneapolis to be with her sister, Margaret, Henrietta accepted a position as a chemistry teacher at the Central High School. During her stay there, she began a Bible study for young people at the First Baptist Church (Fidelis Class) comprising small groups, a minimum of five girls to a maximum of ten with a leader, which grew to 3,000 attendees in 10 years. After the 10 years of managing the First Baptist Church Sunday school, Henrietta took a sabbatical year to seek full-time Christian work. She then visited the First Presbyterian Church in Hollywood, California, where she met with Dr Stewart MacLennan, the residing pastor, and was offered a full-time position as Director of Christian Education – a position she faithfully managed for 35 years. In this new role, she was put in charge of training Sunday School teachers, but her curriculum included everyone, from children to adults. She was known to impact thousands of people with biblical principles of outstanding wisdom with humour and optimism.

She acquired such traits from her father, who was a visionary with an extraordinary capacity to train people for his banking business, and her grandmother's ideas through her upbringing from her enthusiastic God-fearing mother.

She practised a one-on-one evangelistic approach with young people in Bible study and teacher-training programmes, hence increasing the Sunday School attendance of the First Presbyterian Church from about 450 to more than 6000 young people within two years, making it the largest Sunday School of its time.

She continued to attract thousands more through her teaching , which equipped, empowered and led many young people to faith in Christ – who went on in turn to lead a lot more lives to Christ. Her consistent service of winning souls and her significant impact on evangelical Christianity earned her the nickname 'mother of modern evangelism'. She co-founded the National Sunday School Association and became well-known as one of the most influential Christian leaders and great mentors of the $20^{th}$ century.

All her ministry achievements were attributed to her total dependency on and trust in God and her fervent prayers. She made every student feel like 'the most important person in the whole world', in a welcoming study environment. Her inspiring Bible teaching and the relevance of the message to people's lives attracted more people to seek God.

Her extensive knowledge and understanding of biblical text influenced more Christian organisations and leaders such as Billy Graham, Jim Rayburn, Dawson Trotman and Bill Bright, founder of Campus Crusade for Christ, to become full-time ministers of the gospel.

Henrietta Mears founded the non-denominational Forest Home Christian Conference Centre in California, with a conviction that Christian camps transform lives, saying, *'A week at camp will accomplish spiritually in a student's life what it takes years to do otherwise.* 'Forest Home welcomes people from all denominations to come and encounter Jesus and experience transformation through retreats and Christian educational events and activities. Hundreds of decisions of commitment to Christ have been recorded over the years in a Book of Remembrance kept at the centre.

With calculated foresight, Henrietta established her own publishing company, Gospel Light Publications, to print and preserve her training materials, including her guidelines for running Sunday Schools effectively and productively. It is estimated that she sold hundreds of thousands of copies of her curricula. Her book *What the Bible is All About* sold over four million copies. Her in-depth spiritual background, prayer and hard work were influenced by her upbringing through her mother's disciplined daily devotions of Bible reading, prayer and her passion in sharing the gospel with people around her. This fulfils the scripture to *'train a child in the way he should go, and when he is old he will not turn from it'* (Proverbs 22:6). The goal of her ministry was to *'teach the Word clearly and correctly to the end, that people may come to know Christ as Saviour and Lord and to grow spiritually, faithful in every good work'*, echoing Ephesians 2:10.

Even though vocational ministry opportunities for women were limited in her time, Henrietta rose above the norm and proved her biblical understanding of male leadership and not male domination in her ministry.

She was best known as the innovative and dynamic Director of Christian Education. Her message was Christ-centred and practical for all. She was awarded an honorary Doctor of Humanities degree by Bob Jones university, on the basis of her remarkable contributions to Christian education. As her outstanding legacy and influence continues to impact some two generations after her passing in 1963, one writer in Christianity Today (Zoba,1996) called her '*the grandmother of us all*'.

## MOTHER TERESA (1910-1997)

Mother Teresa, the Catholic Albanian, was born Agnes Gonxha Bojaxhiu in Skopje, in the Republic of Macedonia, on August 26th, 1910. She lost her father at age eight and was raised by her mother. At 12, she felt a calling to devote her life to God. She left her parental home at age 18 and joined the Sisters of Loreto in Ireland, with missions intent. After a few months of training in Dublin, she was sent to India, where she took her first vows as a nun and chose to be called Sister Mary Teresa, after Saint Teresa of Lisieux, a patron saint of missionaries – her inspiration for her future ministry.

Mother Teresa taught at St Mary's High School in Calcutta for 17 years. Whilst a teacher, she felt a second calling from God to care for the sick and help the poor in her community. On the basis of that, and by her faith and obedience to God, she sought permission from her superiors to leave the convent school to follow her passion and God's calling on her life.

She devoted herself to working full time with the sick, the 'poorest of the poor', and started open-air schools for children in the slums of Calcutta with no funds, depending on divine provision. She was soon joined by voluntary helpers, then financial support started coming in as a confirmation that God equips the called. Her determination, tenacity, courage and faith in her calling as a missionary paved the way for her to start her own order, The Missionaries of Charity, with permission from the Holy See, in October 1950, with the fundamental task of loving and caring for the poor, marginalised, deprived, abandoned and unloved in society. The Society eventually became an International Religious Family by a decree of Pope Paul VI. This enabled Mother Teresa to extend the scope of her missions. They built homes for orphans, nursing homes for the destitute and lepers and free hospices for the terminally ill in Calcutta. A former US Senator, Mark Hatfield, visited Mother Teresa's 'Kalighat Home of the Pure Heart', formerly known as the 'Kalighat Home for the Dying'. Witnessing the magnitude of the suffering and the burden on the hands of Mother Teresa and her co-workers, he asked, *'How can you bear the load without being crushed beneath it?* Mother Teresa replied, *'My dear Senator, I am not called to be successful, I am called to be faithful.'* The Missionaries of Charity gave every patient the opportunity to die with dignity according to the rituals of their faith: Muslims were read the Quran, Hindus received water from the Ganges, and Christians received Last Rites. However, Mother Teresa was known to encourage members of her order to baptise dying patients. *'A beautiful death,'* she said, *'is for people who lived like animals to die like angels – loved and wanted.'*

She devoted her entire life to serving humanity and honouring God, for: *'Religion that God our father accepts as pure and faultless is this: to look after orphans and widows in their distress and keep oneself from being polluted by the world'* (James 1:27).

She was nicknamed the 'saint of the slums' and 'mother of all mothers' to the numerous orphans. She nurtured every life with compassion, loving-kindness and joy. This fulfils the scripture:

*'Sing, barren woman,*
*you who never bore a child;*
*burst into song, shout for joy,*
*you who were never in labour;*
*because more are the children of the desolate woman*
*than of her who has a husband,'*
*says the Lord.*
*Isaiah 54:1*

The gospel message of grace, mercy, compassion and sacrifice was very evident in her ministry. She received a number of awards, both in India and internationally in recognition of her good works; including the Nobel Peace Prize in 1979 for her outstanding work of helping humanity with her missionary work. She generously donated all the prize money of 192,000 dollars to the poor in India. The legacy of her missionary charities still functions in more than 40 countries with about 4,000 nuns and thousands of lay workers. With her last words, 'I can't breathe!', she departed the earth and went to be with the Lord on 5$^{th}$ September 1997.

She was canonised as Saint Teresa of Calcutta on September 4, 2016, by Pope Frances I.

## NANNY OF THE MAROONS (1686-1760)

Nanny was not a missionary, but a courageous woman who willingly devoted her life to defend and speak for those who could not speak for themselves. She physically fought to secure their freedom (see Proverbs 31:8-9 and John 15:13). She is Jamaica's only female national heroine, honourably described as 'The Right Excellent Nanny of the Maroons'. She was born in West Africa into the Ashanti tribe of Ghana. As a child, she and several of her relatives, including her siblings Accompong, Cugjoe, Jonny and Quou, were sold as slaves after being captives of tribal wars in their homeland, and taken to Jamaica.

Nanny and her four brothers managed to escape from the plantations of their slave masters. They fought for their freedom and formed maroon communities that were named after them, including Nanny Town in Jamaica.

Nanny became the leader of the Jamaican Maroons at the beginning of the $18^{th}$ century. Her exceptional leadership qualities and strong influence on her people gained her the description of 'Queen Nanny', 'Granny Nanny' or 'Nanny of the Maroons'. She was a symbol of unity and strength for her people and was known for her bravery, charisma and wisdom. Her image is on the Jamaican $500, which is mostly referred to as a 'Nanny'.

Her prowess as a witty military leader with masterful camouflages and tactical concealments aided her victories during the first maroon war, which lasted for several years until a peace treaty was signed with the British colonisers on $20^{th}$ April 1740. This treaty stopped the hostilities and recognised freedom, granting 500 acres of land to Nanny and her followers. Nanny's skills in organising guerrilla warfare caused the British years of significant losses. With the help of her brothers and her military forces, she made several military raids to free about 1000 slaves from the plantations and settled them in the maroon communities. She worked hard to ensure that the Windward Maroons thrived as a strong community with freedom, dignity and independence as their rightful inheritance.

Through the power of words, God brought order to the world (Genesis 1:1-25). Jesus also taught that you shall have what you say by faith (Mark 11:23). Again, one can only receive the grace of salvation by confessing the Lord Jesus with one's mouth (Romans 10:9). Furthermore, the Bible commands us to decree something and it shall be established unto us (Job 22:28). The tongue (words), therefore, has the power of life and death, and those who love it will eat its fruits (Proverbs 18:21). This was the basic concept of the courageous and inspiring songs Nanny taught her followers. The words were intended to boost their confidence amid crises. The maroons chanted some of these songs at war times, which proved powerful to keep away the British troops who attempted to penetrate the mountain to overpower them.

Nanny's brashness and tenacity, as well as her leadership style, reflected the judge and prophetess Deborah (Judges 4 and 5). She also acted like Sheerah, the daughter of Ephraim, who took the security of her family seriously because of raiders who murdered her older brothers. She avoided tents and built solid walls of protection, so that their enemies could not penetrate to harm them as they had done in the past. She built the three towns of Lower and Upper Beth Horon, as well as Uzzen Sheerah (1 Chronicles 7:20-24).

Nanny's boldness was also akin to her younger tribal descendant, Nana Yaa Asantewa, the brave and charismatic Ashanti queen mother. Nana Yaa Asantewa was chosen by the regional Ashanti kings in 1900 as the spiritual and military head. She led the 5,000 strong national Ashanti army in a fight to prevent the British governor-general, Frederick Hodgson, unreasonably demanding the Asante golden stool, a sacred symbol of the Asante Region. Nana Yaa Asantewa, a role-model of dynamic female leadership, once dared the men in her region with her famous and enthralling statement:

> *... Is it true that the bravery of the Ashanti is no more? I cannot believe it. It cannot be! I must say this, if you the men of Ashanti will not go forward, then we will. We the women will. I shall call upon my fellow women. We will fight the white men. We will fight till the last of us falls in the battlefields.*

The maroons worshipped a god they called Nyankopong or Yankipon, which is the exact name that the Akans in Ghana call the only one true God Almighty; meaning 'great friend'. Nanny's outstanding prowess, achievements and mysterious supernatural powers of catching bullets and redirecting them back to opponents who shot her were all attributed to Obeah, which is associated with both good and bad magical charms and mysticism in general.

The Bible says that all things are possible to those who believe, and Nanny is no exception to this statement. She undoubtedly believed in her African god, Nyankopong, who is also known as Nyame – meaning fulfilling, dependable or satisfying – to supernaturally help her combat the colonial forces. The colonial army usually came against the Maroons in organised factions, but were often overpowered by Nanny's strategic manoeuvres with her troops.

Nanny actively factored in God, in her undertakings through the medium of her ancestral spirits by the pouring of libations to her god, 'Nyankopong'. Her God did not leave nor forsake her in the realms of the supernatural when she needed the strength to wage wars. She was undoubtedly protected, guided and aided both naturally and supernaturally to prevail victoriously over her strong enemies who rather trusted in horses and chariots (Psalm 20:7-8).

In the act of libation, as practiced by the maroons, and Africans in general, a drink or water in a container, usually a calabash, is lifted up towards the heavens with the saying: 'Almighty God, we show you drink but we don't offer you drink.' Then the drink is poured onto the ground for 'Asaase Efua', the goddess of the earth, as a tribute with prayers of thanksgiving and petition.

Nanny's legacy is a great inspiration for racial justice, civil rights, freedom from oppression and domination, equality, courage, resilience and self-confidence.

## ROSA PARKS (1913-2005)

Rosa was well referred to as the 'mother of the modern-day civil rights movement'. She was a seamstress by profession and also a civil rights activist, who came into the limelight for her refusal to give up her seat on the bus for a white male. She was arrested for civil disobedience, which triggered the massive Montgomery Bus Boycott in the USA. In her book *Quiet Strength,* Rosa acknowledged God for her bravery on that historic day, saying, *'I felt the Lord would give me the strength to endure whatever I had to face. God did away with all my fears... it was time for someone to stand up, or in my case sit down. I refused to move.'*

## JONI EARECKSON-TADA (15 October 1949)

Joni Eareckson-Tada is an evangelical Christian author, artist, radio host and conference speaker. At age 17, in July 1967, Joni had a diving accident and sustained a severe spinal cord injury, which rendered her quadriplegic and confined to a wheelchair. During her two-year convalescence and rehabilitation, Joni redirected her anger, depression, suicidal thoughts and religious doubts by expressing herself on paper through learning to paint with a brush between her teeth. She also started to write that way but eventually resorted to voice recognition software. She has written over 50 books about disability and Christianity, including her autobiography, which has been translated into 38 languages. She signs all her paintings 'P.T.L.', which stands for 'Praise the Lord'.

Joni has worked phenomenally hard and touched thousands of people through her disability ministry, with all the difficulties this entails including bodily aches and chronic pain, which she describes as 'jaw-splitting'. She has said that her ongoing bodily pain reminds her of the gruesome cup of Jesus's Gethsemane experience – nevertheless, in the Father's perfect will. The thought of this consoles her and motivates her to constantly speak to her pain with scripture, by *'simple faith and with wilful determined thanks'*. This is her way of yielding to God in her despair.

In addition to this, Joni has gone through breast cancer diagnosis and treatment, for which she is in remission to the glory of God. Her amazingly brave demeanour profusely exudes hope to the hopeless, strength to the weary and courage to the broken-hearted. She consistently showcases an awesome God who takes our brokenness and makes something beautiful out of broken vessels. He gives beauty for ashes, and His strength is made perfect in weakness, as Joni constantly testifies to: *'Deny your weakness and you will never know God's strength in you'*. Her selfless and sacrificial lifestyle is indeed inspiring and a blessing to all the lives she touches with her ministry (see 2 Corinthians 4:7; 12:9).

In 1979, she founded the 'Joni and Friends' organisation to extend hope, humanitarian resources, financial support, and the message of the gospel of Jesus Christ to the jaded, the vulnerable and those who are despondent after tragedies, losses and unexplained circumstances in their lives. The 'Joni and Friends' radio programme teaches and encourages listeners with scriptures and helps them become more aware of what it is like to live with a disability.

Joni's non-profit-making organisation runs annual camp retreats, respite care, crisis response and getaways for families who are affected by disabilities. The organisation also collects, repairs and distributes new wheelchairs and other mobility devices for both adults and children nationally and globally through its 'Wheels for the World' ministry, which has donated about 200,000 wheelchairs to the disabled. President Ronald Reagan of the USA granted that Joni be part of the National Council on Disability (NCD), which empowers individuals with disabilities and promotes equal opportunities through policies and recommendations.

There is also the Joni's House ministry – international disability centres in some of the poorest parts of the world, in answer to the Luke 14:21 and 23 mandate to *'Go out quickly into the streets and alleys of the town and bring in the poor, the crippled, the blind and the lame… Go out to the roads and country lanes and make them come in, so that my house will be full.'* Joni's House provides shelters and safe haven for families with special needs. They are helped to find hope, dignity and comfort through spiritual resources of prayers and Bible teachings. Physical acts of kindness, love and compassion are also rendered.

The centres also provide a welcoming environment for emotional healing and aim to break the barriers of exclusion, exploitation and stigmatisation of the disabled. They also offer training that eventually enable artisans to earn a living to support themselves and their families.

God has used Joni's life-changing accident, and the challenging adjustment to her present way of life, to encourage the discouraged, comfort the weary, bless the needy in diverse ways and most of all to draw lost souls to His kingdom of love. Joni's unwavering faith in the Lord and her remarkable achievements for the world of disability are immeasurably profound. She undoubtedly fulfils the scripture that she can do all things through Christ who enables her with His power, wisdom and strength.

## JOYCE MEYER (4 June 1943)

Joyce Meyer was born Pauline Joyce Hutchison in South St. Louis in 1943. She was born again at age nine but was not fully committed until her apparent 'Damascus Road' experience when she was praying intensely while driving to work one morning in 1976. She heard God call her name, and she felt loved the whole day – which, she says, made her feel like she was 'drunk with the Spirit of God'. Joyce's unusual encounter with the Holy Spirit that day eventually led to her powerful ministry of forgiveness, forbearance and release, under the banner of 'Enjoying Everyday Life'.

Joyce uses her own life experience as a victim of sexual abuse by her father to preach forgiveness and God's redemption to her audience. After going through years of hurt and resentment against both parents, as her mother could not seem to stop her father's indecent advances, Joyce chose to allow the Holy Spirit to help her to forgive her parents. Her willingness and obedience to God's command on forgiveness, as Jesus taught His disciples in the Lord's Prayer – *'if you forgive other people when they sin against you, your heavenly Father will also forgive you'* (Matthew 6:12,14) – and also the lessons from the parable of the unforgiving servant, aided her to forgive them (Matthew 18:21-35).

She subsequently took over the full care of her parents by providing them with shelter, food, clothing, and medical care, and delightfully led them to Christ before their passing.

Joyce's painful test has now become her testimony of release and hope for multitudes of people, especially victims of abuse, to relate to the peace of the Lord that passes all understanding and the power of forgiveness that sets the captive free. Joyce simply admonishes that unforgiveness can become a heavy burden on one's spirit and can leave one with no strength, which consequently depresses the soul and grieves the Holy Spirit. She therefore encourages her hearers to release all pain, hatred, bitterness, anger and any resentment they feel against people into the hands of God for the liberty and restoration only He can give. *'For the Lord is the Spirit, and wherever the Spirit of the Lord is, there is freedom* (2 Corinthians 3:17, see also Ephesians 4:30-32 Matthew 5:23-24; Romans 12:19).

## LIZ CARTER (31 December 1971)

Liz Carter was born in Northampton, UK. As a child, she yearned to be an author, and at age eight, she wrote her first book. It took a fair while for her to get back into her passion of writing due to a chronic lung disease which causes her much pain and keeps her housebound for long periods, with regular hospitalisations. She is a wife and mother to two children, and lives in Wellington, Shropshire, with her husband, a vicar in the Church of England. Even though her chronic illness has been a constant struggle throughout her life, she has learnt to keep the faith and hope in the Lord for her sustenance and healing. Her absolute trust in God for daily living has been a source of strength, comfort, and peace that passes human judgment.

Liz's resilience in maintaining a positive spirit of *'I can do everything through Him who gives me strength'* propelled her beyond the classroom, as a teacher, into her God-assigned purpose in due time. By faith, she caught her 'mantle' of a skilful 'writer's pen' in her capacity as a first-class degree holder in theology and now living her childhood dream as a renowned author. She writes both fiction and non-fiction materials and has been a resident poet for her local town. She works as a freelance editor and designer, with great creativity and skilful content. God's purpose will always come to pass, no matter how long it takes. *'For the revelation awaits an appointed time; it speaks at the end and will not prove false. Though it linger, wait for it; it will certainly come and it will not delay'* (Habakkuk 2:3).

Liz incorporates her writings with study guide videos, in which she passionately shares the love of God, the hope that Jesus offers mankind, and also comforts with the comfort that she herself receives in her struggles (see 2 Corinthians 1:3-5; 1 Peter 5:7). She views her life as an adventure with the covenant-keeping God, who said, *'I have loved you with an everlasting love; I have drawn you with loving-kindness'* (Jeremiah 31:3).

The Bible reassures us that:

> *Nothing can separate us from the love of God; neither death nor life, neither angels nor demons, neither the present nor the future, nor any powers, neither height*

> *nor depth, nor anything else in all creation, will be able to separate us from the love of God that is in Christ Jesus our Lord.*
> *Romans 8:35-39*

Even though sometimes she wonders where God is when it hurts so much, her belief that God's love and grace allows the believer to be a conqueror in adversity is sufficient for her to keep standing. She testifies about God's faithfulness in her ups and downs and encourages her listeners to keep keeping on and see the salvation of the Lord in their uncertainties. An example of such encouraging clips, which I have followed, is 'Catching Contentment: A Six Session Bible Study Course'.

Liz took her inspiration for writing her book 'Catching Contentment' from the apostle Paul's exhortation to the Philippians to rejoice always – his secret of contentment while he was under house arrest with armed guards, as illustrated in Philippians 4:4-13. Based on her own experiences and her faith, Liz shares that contentment is a choice and can be found not only in perfection, but one can know contentment in spite of their struggles, loss, sicknesses, disappointments, pain and even in confinements, as she recalls her own experiences of hospitalisations and also shielding away from her family in lockdown.

Liz's life is an inspiration for the weary to find solace, the sick to be patient in affliction and persistent in prayer, and the disabled to be joyful in hope and know that they are not alone.

## ARABA NKRANSEMA TAYLOR (April 1923 – May 2023)

Araba Nkransema Taylor was born in Winneba, Ghana, on April 10 1923, to Araba Baffoa and Samuel Kofi Esilfie Taylor, all of blessed memory. This welcoming and compassionate woman represents all the unsung and unnamed female heroines in this narrative. Araba Nkransema's charitable deeds and kind-hearted attitude, with her empathetic and heart-first approach towards people, came from her desire to honour God. Araba would often go out of her way to seek the welfare of others and accept them for who they were. She was always delighted to share her ideas, experiences and material possessions with her family and friends alike. She went beyond her usual vocation of welcoming babies into the world to embracing the needy and bringing them into her own space to care for them as she would her own family. Such unique traits of outstanding human relations and inclusion earned Araba the nickname 'Auntie Mama' as she acted as a mother to all.

Araba Nkransema's caring attitude motivated her career choice as a nurse-midwife, a vocation she initially shadowed as a teenager with her maternal grandmother, Nana Adwoa Gyatowa, a traditional midwife, before formally training for her certification.

With her conservative Christian background, Araba built her life on basic Christian principles and looked to Christ as her hope and stay. She nurtured her own children, as well as every child in her care, with lessons from her own life experiences and with the biblical ethos of *'training a child in the way he should go, and when he is old he will not turn from it'.*

She mindfully sought and demonstrated peace by being the one who would often mediate in raging situations, uncomfortable circumstances and unhealthy relationships, both physically and prayerfully, for a peaceful resolve. She avowed from her own life experience that one's positive impact on people does leave an indelible and rewarding memory: as rightly quoted by Maya Angelo, *'People will forget what you said and what you did. But people will never forget how you made them feel.'*

Araba also believed and shared the fact that God blesses us to be the dispensers of His blessings to others. She therefore upheld that *'we should not become weary of doing good, for at the proper time we will reap a harvest if we do not give up'* (Galatians 6:9). Another strong belief of hers, which she would often voice out in her native language, was *'eye obi dze yie a, woso wodze ye yie'*, meaning *'what you make happen for others, God would make happen to you'* (Luke 6:31). For *'He who refreshes others will himself be refreshed'* (Proverbs 11:25), and *'With the measure you use, it will be measured to you'* (Luke 6:38b).

These and many more scriptural ethics fuelled her passion as a widow in her early fifties to feed, clothe, willingly accommodate and financially support people. This continued into her eighties as a pensioner, until her demise at one hundred. She considered her generosity as casting her bread upon the waters (Ecclesiastes 11:1), and she found fulfilment as people felt helped. Such a faith-filled attitude portrayed her as an outstanding benevolent figure to her family and her community.

As an active member of her local Methodist church, Madam Araba's contribution of service – physically, spiritually and financially – to honour the work of the Lord, was her paramount act of worship, including the annual thank-offerings on her birthdays. She never left her bedroom or her house in the morning without praying with the aid of devotional books like Daily Bread and The Word for Today by Bob and Debby Gass.

Her Bible was the most worn-out book at her bedside, with other books like *Good Morning Holy Spirit* by Benny Hinn, *The Power of a Praying Parent and Woman* by Stormie Omartian, *God's Secret Agents* by Billy Graham, *The Pilgrim's Progress* by John Bunyan, and a lot more biblical literature which aided her to pray expectantly.

Like the virtuous woman in Proverbs 31, Araba Nkransema was a wise investor in her occupation as a carer and in people's well-being and education. She ensured that everyone she was involved with benefited from a skill, either through her advice or financial assistance.

As a skilled nurse-midwife, she worked diligently with her own hands and paid attention to detail for quality outcomes, with her own uniquely worded motto of *'brighten the corner where you are'*. Her calculated and remarkable business acumen motivated her decision to retire early from the government hospital to establish her own midwifery and clinical practice. She consequently bought a privately owned maternity home from a colleague. Araba centred her practice on the health and well-being of women and children. The establishment generated employment and basic training for the young women in her community who aspired to become professional healthcare workers, with tremendous results.

At her maternity and clinical practice, 'Auntie Mama' allowed the parents unable to afford maternity bills to go home with their babies with her heartfelt blessing, coupled with the strong conviction that *'God meant it for good'* (Genesis 50:20, see also Proverbs 31:20). She believed that situations like these do not 'just happen' and that, in due course, God works it all out for the good of the people who love Him (Romans 8:28).

Nine of her family members have proudly named their ten children – nine girls and one boy – after her. Her very first namesake, Araba Nkransema Ocrane, is usually referred to as 'Auntie Mama', in her honour. Young Auntie Mama chose the professional path of her grandmother, Araba Nkransema, and is now a highly respected nurse-midwife and a manager in her health organisation in Agona Swedru, Ghana.

During her 99th birthday celebration, when Araba was asked by her pastor about the secret of her graceful old age, she humorously blamed it on all the people who kept saying 'God bless you' for the 'little things' that she did for them.

Her general communications were full of wisdom, scriptural words of encouragement and sincere gratitude. She often responded to the question of her well-being with *'Nyame n'adom'* (by God's grace). Her favourite songs included *All Things Bright and Beautiful, The Lord's My Shepherd,* and *To God be the Glory.*

Araba Nkransema's 'Jabez prayer' to the Lord was a request to bless her with 100 healthy years, to be around for her children, grandchildren and everyone she had taken in as her own. The Lord graciously granted her request, and on April 23 2023 she celebrated a grand centennial birthday thanksgiving with her family from around the world. Despite her physical limitations with old age, Araba was still *compos mentis* at 100 years old and could fairly engage in pleasant and humorous conversations. She was very much aware and appreciated all the well wishes for her centennial birthday, including a special message from His Royal Highness Prince William of the United Kingdom; his *'heartfelt congratulations and his sincere thoughts for her special year'*, with his photo attached.

Araba Nkransema Taylor fulfilled her earthly assignment with poise, hope and serenity, thus demonstrating she was a blessing and great asset to the Gyatowa and Taylor families of Winneba and the Agbolegbe and Avevor families of Atito and Anloga in Ghana. This leaves her dear family with no other words than to call her their quintessential heroine.

# MOTHERHOOD: EVERY WOMAN'S MINISTRY

The noble ministry of motherhood is a God-ordained calling for every woman (biological, adoptive or spiritual), through Christ, to draw sons and daughters to Him *'from whom every family in heaven and on earth derives its name'* (Ephesians 3:15).

Women are fearfully and wonderfully created by God, in Christ, to do good works He prepared in advance for them to do, including the command to be *'fruitful and increase in number: fill the earth and subdue it'* (Genesis 1:28); to nurture and *'train up a child in the way he should go, and when he is old he will not turn from it'* (Proverbs 22:6).

However, God does not give the gift of biological children to every woman, but in His sovereignty, He reassures the woman unable to conceive, as in these words through the prophet Isaiah:

> *Sing, O barren woman, you who never bore a child: burst into song, shout for joy, you who were never in labour; because more are the children of the desolate woman than of her who has a husband.*
> *Isaiah 54:1*

This passage teaches that God sets the boundaries for our lives; therefore, if the barrenness of a woman is His will, then He has a purpose to use the situation for His ultimate glory and for the good of those who love Him and are called according to His purpose (Romans 8:28). For the same God who sets the lonely in families also *'settles the childless woman in her home as a happy mother of children'* (Psalms 68:6, 113:9).

A mother is a female parent, foster parent, guardian, step-mother or mentor whose creation and nature as a 'helpmeet' in God's image enable her to nurture, love, nourish, teach, support, empower, correct, encourage, and comfort (as God; Isaiah 66:13). She raises up the children that God has gifted her as a heritage and a reward to His glory (Genesis 1:27, 2:18; Psalm 127:3-5).

Motherhood, therefore, is God's gift and a blessing with a biblical responsibility to instil His word in the children that He formed in the womb:

> *Teach them to your children, talk about them when you sit at home and when you walk along the road, when you lie down and when you get up. Write them on the doorframes of your houses and on your gates, so that your days and the days of your children may be many in the land the Lord swore to give your ancestors, as many as the days that the heavens are above the earth.*
>
> *Deuteronomy 11:18-21*

The knowledge of God's Word will prepare and equip the believing family to give an answer to everyone who asks them to give the reason for the hope that they have, but with gentleness and respect (1 Peter 3:15; Hosea 4:6).

In his letter to Titus, Paul, who addressed him as *'my true son in our common faith',* also encouraged him, as the leader, *'to teach the older women to be reverent in the way they live',* so they would lead by example in training and teaching the younger women in godly womanhood and honour of God (Titus 2:3-5).

Again, Paul commended Eunice and Lois for the impact their sincere Christian faith had on Timothy, and admonished him to do his best to avoid godless chatter but rather present himself to God *'as one approved, a worker who does not need to be ashamed and who correctly handles the word of truth'* (2 Timothy 1:5; 2:15). Timothy, whom Paul called '*my son*', lived up to his name, *'honouring God'*, and went along with Paul on missions to win souls for the kingdom of God.

The ministry of motherhood also encourages parents and guardians, like wailing women, to travail in prayer until the will of God is done for their children, families, the church and the nation (Jeremiah 9:17-20). For *'God knows our troubles and our wandering; stores all our tears in a bottle, has counted each one of them, and they are recorded in the Book'* (Psalm 56:8). Jesus witnessed many tears and acknowledged them during His earthly ministry, including the painful wailing at His crucifixion by His followers (Luke 7:12-13, 44, 8:52, 23:28; John 20:15). He wept over Jerusalem for failing to recognise Him as Prince of Peace and not being prepared for her Saviour (Luke 19:41-44). As our High Priest in the order of

Melchizedek, *'He offered up prayers and petitions with fervent cries and tears to the one who could save him from death, and he was heard because of his reverent submission'* (Hebrews 5:7); indicating His care and love for mankind.

A mother's sincere prayer offered in faith, in spirit and in truth, would break through with tremendous power to derail any obstacles facing the family. Strongholds and spiritual prison walls are broken, healing takes place, the prodigals come home, restoration takes place and freedom is wrought by the power of the Holy Spirit (James 1:13-15; 2 Corinthians 3:17).

The Bible says that Satan, the adversary, *'prowls around like a roaring lion looking for someone to devour'.* He assumes all sorts of attractive guises to entice children, as he would to any disloyal subjects who follow his ways and systems. He is nicknamed the 'prince of this world', 'the deceiver' and 'the accuser'. He accuses the brethren before God, day and night, to emphasise their wrongdoings and to break their fellowship with God. However, he is subordinate to God and can only do what God in His supremacy will permit, as demonstrated in Job 1:6-12 and Zechariah 3:1-4. He only gets his way if man, in his selfish nature, chooses to be a lawful captive to him through disobedience and lustful desires. Yet God the merciful Father reassures us that:

> *Even the captives of the mighty warriors will be taken from them, and the blunder retrieved from the fierce; I will contend with those who contend with you, and your children I will save... Then all mankind will*

> *know that I, the LORD, am your Saviour, your Redeemer, the Mighty One of Jacob.*
> *Isaiah 49:24-26*

Furthermore, through His steadfast love, God has made us complete in Christ, who is the Head over every power and authority; He disarmed and made a public spectacle of them, triumphing over them by the cross (Colossians 2:10,15). God has also:

> *… Exalted Him to the highest place and gave Him the name that is above every name, that at the name of Jesus every knee should bow, in heaven and on earth and under the earth, and every tongue confess that Jesus is Lord, to the glory of God the Father.*
> *Philippians 2:9-11*

The ministry of motherhood illustrates God's love through parenting, mentoring, fostering and spiritual mothering. Bringing up children safely and successfully must be executed in love with affection, patience and tenderness to enable them to trust, listen and willingly adhere to sound parental instruction and teaching (Proverbs 1:8-9). God's unconditional love protects, yet does not withhold life-shaping discipline from His children, because *'folly is bound up in the heart of a child, but the rod of discipline* (not punishment nor abuse) *will drive it far away, and impart wisdom'* (Proverbs 22:15). *'No discipline seems pleasant at the time, but painful. Later on, however, it produces a harvest of righteousness and peace for those who have been trained by it. But a child left to himself disgraces his mother'* (Hebrews 12:11; Proverbs 29:15,17). The Bible teaches not to *'exasperate your children, instead, bring them up in the training and the instruction of the Lord'* (Ephesians 6:4).

Jesus also warned, *'If anyone causes one of these little ones – those who believe in me – to stumble, it would be better for them to have a large millstone hang around their neck and be drowned in the depth of the sea'* (Matthew 18:6).

Motherhood as a ministry provides safe havens for children, binds families together and creates an accessible environment for warmth, compassion, guidance and unrestricted love that allays a child's fears, eases their distress and soothes their emotional disturbances. Such an atmosphere of kindness, inclusion, respect, care, and liberty exudes irresistible power, which even the most rebellious child cannot obliterate. Bonding is also established, which boosts self-confidence and promotes security.

Scientists from the American Association for the Advancement of Science have reported that mothers and their babies can synchronise their heartbeats by just looking at each other's face. Denzel Washington said, *'A mother is a son's first true love, and a son is his mother's last true love.'* The Lord Jesus Christ demonstrated such love at the cross when He handed over the care of His mother to John, the disciple He loved, before His death (John 19:25-27). God has used the analogy of a mother's close bond to her children to describe how much He cares and unconditionally loves His children, through the prophet Isaiah: *'Can a mother forget the baby at her breast and have no compassion on the child she has borne? Though she may forget, I will not forget you!'* (Isaiah 49:15).

There is no perfection in parenting. Marie Angélique Arnauld, a French abbess and religious influence, once stated: *'Perfection is not doing the extraordinary things, but is doing ordinary things extraordinarily well.'* Perfection, however, dwells with God, the creator, from whom our sufficiency comes. He has given everyone the ability to do certain things uniquely well, and the Holy Spirit works in the surrendered soul who is obedient to God's timing and seasons and willing to accomplish God's purposes (Philippians 2:13, Isaiah 1:19). By the grace of God, a mother can intuitively figure out how to mould her children morally, socially, spiritually and intellectually, despite every child being born with unique personalities and abilities. She naturally possesses the insight (or 'hunch') that guides her to take courageous initiative in her children's situations that they may not foresee.

Motherhood involves sacrifices, labour, tears, gains, loss and a multitasking ability. A mother takes it all on board, paid and unpaid 24/7, as a helpmeet or as a sole breadwinner to make ends meet. However, motherhood is extremely rewarding since the products being nurtured are God's good and perfect gifts to the custodians. Counting such a noble 'chore' as a blessing would encourage one to be on the same page as Joshua, who, in the midst of carrying the enormous task of shepherding God's people, boldly declared, *'But as for me and my household, we will serve the LORD,'* as his chief end of glorifying God (Joshua 24:15).

# CONCLUSION

Within Christianity, a ministry is an assignment or office held by an individual or a group of people elected by ecclesiastical authority or a calling by God (divine appointment), to serve the Lord and humanity. People undertaking such ministries include benefactors, philanthropists, youth leaders and, in the body of Christ: pastors, apostles, prophets, deacons, intercessors, evangelists, lay preachers, worship leaders, Sunday School teachers, house-group leaders, administrators and so on (1 Corinthians 12:28; Ephesians 4:11-13). These offices require love, focus, humility, sacrifice, integrity, dedication, surrender to God and loyalty to the people being served (Micah 6:8).

In Jesus' earthly ministry, He chose twelve apostles out of His disciples to learn from Him and to assist Him in establishing the kingdom of Heaven here on earth, by preaching the good news. He gave them the authority to cast out unclean spirits, heal the sick and raise the dead (Matthew 10:1-4; Mark 3:13-19; Luke 6:13-16; see also Acts 6:1-4). The apostles (eleven) were later commissioned in the same vein to take the gospel to the ends of the world, along with all other believers including women *(to go and bear fruit – fruit that will last)* and to go on to lead the church (Matthew 28:16-20; Mark 16:14-18; John 15:16; Acts 1:8).

There is a well-known quote by Brigham Young: *'If you educate a man, you educate an individual. But if you educate a woman, you educate a nation.'* This famous quote has been explored in an article I once read, 'The Life of a Maasai Woman' by the Maasai Girls' Education organisation in Kenya. The study found that the women not only gave their time towards their jobs but also spent around 90% of their income on their families and communities, compared with the 35% that an educated man would spend. Such selfless sacrifices by the women were found to reduce poverty, improve health, promote sound minds and provide more education.

Empowering women with God's Word, as the Lord Jesus and the apostles did, promotes their spiritual growth and enables them to impact their sphere of influence. In their role as parents and guardians, women especially raise God-fearing families with the truths they live by, as charity is said to begin at home. It can be recounted that this concept has resonated with most of the women mentioned in this book as true life experiences. The Bible says, '*The fruit of the righteous is a tree of life, and whoever wins souls is wise*' (Proverbs 11:30).

Such fruits are born by abiding in God's Word, as Jesus vividly described in John's gospel, saying, *'I am the vine; you are the branches. If a man remains in me and I in him, he will bear much fruit; apart from me you can do nothing'* (John 15:5).

Passing on the torch of the gospel message to future generations, as these wise women did, brought light into darkness, life to the dead, sight for the blind (physically and spiritually) and hope to the hopeless.

Stronger communities – being each other's keepers – are also promoted in women's ministries, as God does not want mankind to be alone. Therefore, it is vital to pursue one's calling and identify an area of need to reach out and share the love of Jesus through one's gifts and talents. God blesses us to be a blessing. He *'comforts us in all our troubles, so that we can comfort those in any trouble with the comfort we ourselves receive from Him' (2 Corinthians 1:4).*

All the women mentioned in this book lived or are living in this broken world with challenges, trials, opposition, loss, betrayal, conflict and even death. Yet they stood the test of times, rose above their burdens by grace, counted their blessings and boldly said 'yes' to their calling. Like the children of Issachar, most of the women in this narrative understood the times and seasons and were able to discern the promptings of the Holy Spirit and act accordingly. Attitudes echoing David's *'One thing God has spoken, two things I have heard…'* (Psalm 62:11).

God prepared all the wonderful works of these women in advance for them to do in accordance with His will and purpose for their lives. Their good works made them stand out as vessels of God's supremacy, faith-filled believers, God-fearing, God-loving, spiritual mothers, humble-courageous, astute encouragers, symbols of hope, agents of change, role models of future generations and *'good and faithful servants'* to God's glory and His great faithfulness. The Bible sums it all up so beautifully: *'Charm is deceptive, and beauty is fleeting; but a woman who fears the LORD is to be praised'* (Proverbs 31:30).

# APPRECIATION

My sincere gratitude to my beloved husband, Isaac Kweku Mensah, for his great support and confidence in me over the years of our union. His faith in sharing my dream of writing, right from the onset is a testament.

My supportive sons: Jonathan, Richard, Isaac Michael, Christian and my daughter-in-law Ayumi, for their motivation, constructive inputs and enthusiasm.

My cheerleading-nieces: Nana Kwedua Appiah for encouraging the idea of formal writing after hearing a couple of my mini-sermons; Nelly Nkransema Mensah, for inspiring my writing with gentle reminders of *'you have a way with words!',* through our conversations and text messages, and also Joyce Worla Katako for her devotion and kind-hearted care for the family.

To Pastor Isaac Opoku Ware, for his consistent inspiration and constant contributions in directing me towards the path of becoming a writer, as a way of sharing my biblical experiences to bless others – "including myself".

To Rev Martin Ceaser, for recognising the desire in me as an encourager and worshipper, and giving me the opportunity to lead Sunday worship service in Pollards Hill Baptist Church. This led to my enrolment at Spurgeon's College to undertake the Equip To Minister programme, for building my confidence, knowledge and skilful preparation to rightly lead and encourage through the songs of fellowship and the word.

To Liz Carter, for her warmth, patience, kindness and profound expertise in guiding me through my writing as a curious and authentic writer.

# NOTES

# NOTES

# NOTES

# NOTES

Printed in Dunstable, United Kingdom

80111710R00099